dieter rams
the complete works

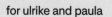for ulrike and paula

dieter rams
the complete works

klaus klemp

foreword

Design is a process, and industrial design is teamwork with many people involved. I have been fortunate to have encountered and worked with many exceptional personalities in my life – at Braun and Vitsœ and also at innumerable conferences and gatherings. There have been so many inspiring conversations with so many people. I have always treasured the global nature of such encounters, because it is only through international dialogue and collaboration that we will be able to shape our world wisely for the future. Any form of nationalism has always been alien to me. We all have different qualities, and the goal has to be to bring them together constructively.

Design is not just about the formal design of our *Dingwelt*, our 'world of things'; it determines the life of every individual and how we all live with one another. Design can promote social togetherness – but it can also damage it. This is why the responsibility carried by designers is so great. Look at all the things we have designed in the last 150 years alone: telephones, cars, radios, televisions, computers and smartphones. Marshall McLuhan was right in saying that the 'medium is the message', in that it both extends and restricts our possibilities.

But I am of the opinion that the key issue here is *how* these extensions are designed. And it will not surprise you when I plead for a degree of restraint in this respect.

Some years ago, I set a series of questions regarding the design of industrial products. We should ask ourselves, for example, whether the product we are designing is really necessary, or if something already exists that does the job well enough, if not better. Does it really help to enrich our lives or does it only appeal to ideas of status? Is it repairable? Is it durable? Easy to use and flexible in its use? Can I master it easily or does the new product dominate me? That last question is one I find particularly relevant today. The primary insight I have gained in my sixty years as a designer, and through my experiences with both companies and end users, is a simple one: 'Less, but better.'

We should surround ourselves with fewer things, but better things. This is not a constraint, it is an advantage, which allows us more space for real life. The same applies to my ten principles of good design – they are not commandments, just a friendly recommendation to think again.

Free yourself from the ballast of too many things. A willingness for order – for simple, calm, restrained forms with longer, more aesthetic, useful lives – seems to me to be of far more importance than constantly trying to invent the next best thing. However, good design does not come through the fulfilment of demands alone. Good everyday design should always be design that speaks for itself. It can seldom succeed, but when it does, special products such as these are a necessary incentive for the design of our whole environment. They are the benchmarks for the future.

'Less, but better' has to hold true for production, but also with respect to short-lived items as well. We have less and less resources, and our rubbish dumps are getting bigger and bigger – even in outer space and in our planet's oceans. We have to protect our climate and we have to design our cities in more intelligent and affordable ways. This is the great challenge of our age for our governments *and* for us in our behaviour as citizens. Last, but not least, we need entrepreneurs and designers to develop intelligent alternatives.

I have always been convinced that good design is a matter for companies and not just individual designers. This conviction has become stronger over the years. Right from the start, my work has been characterized by a focus on the function – the 'use' – of a product in the broadest sense of the word. During this time, the scope of the fields that the word 'function' covers has expanded enormously and we have learned how complex and diverse the function of a product can be. Today we are well aware that the things we make need to have psychological, ecological and social utility as well. The functional, then, has very many facets. But, as far as I can see, there is no alternative.

I am counting on the younger generation, who are hopefully well aware of all these problems and not just concerned with individual advantage and maximum profit. Changing the future was never easy and it has become a lot harder today.

I am convinced that there is an ethics of design – that there *has* to be one. It is time to realize that we have once again reached the end of a phase of disorientation and arbitrariness. Everything seemed possible – and we could do anything we wanted – and the 'me' came before the 'we'. But we have to change our course now – before catastrophe forces us to do so.

'Less, but better' means we must distance ourselves from the *unculture* of excess – of waste. Away from cheapness in the literal, and also the figurative, sense. It also means that we need more things that truly give the buyer and the user what they expect from them: the facilitation, enhancement and strengthening of their lives.

Our task for the future is as follows. We need:

Less and less of the kind of products whose production and use squander resources and are a burden on the environment.

Less and less of the kind of products that stimulate the desire to buy, but are barely used, quickly set aside, thrown away and then replaced with new ones.

Less and less of the kind of products that are nothing more than fashion and become obsolete as soon as that fashion has passed.

Less and less of the kind of products that break quickly, wear out and age prematurely.

In their place we need more and more products that really are – and do – what the buyer and user should expect from them: the facilitation, enhancement and strengthening of our lives.

I believe that one of the most important responsibilities of design – perhaps *the* most important, in respect of society – is to help lighten the chaos that we are forced to live in today.

Let me end with a quote from the Austrian-British philosopher Karl Popper:

'Since we can never know anything for sure, it is simply not worth searching for certainty; but it is well worth searching for truth; and we do this chiefly by searching for mistakes, so that we can correct them.'

I would like to thank all those who have contributed to this catalogue raisonné. First and foremost the author Klaus Klemp, but also all those involved, especially Britte Siepenkothen and the publisher Emilia Terragni.

Dieter Rams

dieter rams – a catalogue raisonné of an industrial designer

This book presents the products and designs of industrial designer Dieter Rams, organized in chronological order from 1947 to 2020. Functioning as a catalogue raisonné, it features everything that Rams has designed as a single work. However, it also includes a curated selection of products made by other members of the Braun design team that Rams oversaw the making of, or was directly involved in. In the case of his own designs, this covers quite a lot. If we take as a starting point every mention of Rams as designer or co-designer in *Braun+Design Collection: 40 Jahre Braun Design – 1955 bis 1995,* the standard reference on Braun design by Jo Klatt and Günter Staeffler from 1995,[1] the number of products he created at Braun during this forty-year period is 514, out of the company's total of 1,272. However, this includes a large number of items to which the adjustments made were merely technical. What is significant is that the designs themselves were not changed, or were only altered very slightly; at Braun, a design was only changed when actual innovations were achieved. This approach reflects a fundamental conviction of Rams and Braun that technical improvements do not automatically warrant a new design, and, as a result, many Braun appliances had an extraordinarily long design cycle. This is in stark contrast to the common business practice of introducing old or barely improved technology to the market packaged in a new look to stimulate consumption. For this reason, the objects presented here only include those that constitute a truly new design. The same rules apply to Rams's designs for Vitsœ; the furniture company continues to sell pieces that first came onto the market in 1960 and 1962, and which have remained virtually unchanged ever since.

This catalogue also covers more than what Rams produced for Braun and Vitsœ, although these were undoubtedly his main fields of activity. During his time as an employee at Braun, Rams had permission to work outside the company, making him, in some respects, a freelancer. Vitsœ was and still is a client for him, one with whom he shares a close and friendly relationship. While his other external projects were few in number, they remain significant to his career, such as his collaboration with the door and window fittings manufacturer Franz Schneider Brakel (FSB).

For this catalogue raisonné, 227 objects were identified in collaboration with Rams, a process that necessitated many an intensive discussion. In addition, there are 50 Braun devices that are either solely or primarily listed under the name of a team member as the creator, but on which Rams had a direct influence. On such example is the playful tail flick he added to Florian Seiffert's mach 2 lighter button (p. 185). While this latter category of products is included in the main chronological sequence, they can be identified by a full-page grey tinted background.

From the spring of 1956 until 1995, two years before he left the company, Rams was head of Braun's design department: initially a small team of three, including Gerd A Müller and Roland Weigend, until it grew to include fifteen members in the 1960s. The word 'head' can also be interpreted literally here, because Rams was perhaps the most reflective of Braun's designers, and he thought about the meaning of his work very early on in his career. Three essential qualities that are often associated with Braun design practice can reasonably be attributed to Rams. First, he was a designer who operated at the highest level of personal productivity; second – and this should not be underestimated – he was a team leader, without whose persistence and diplomacy the company's strong design mentality would not have developed so fully; third and final is the contemplative approach. Rams became a design theorist in the 1970s and argued extensively against

excessive mass consumption and to highlight the environmental destruction it has caused. He has propagated these values in countless publications and lectures worldwide.

From its base in Kronberg, just outside Frankfurt, Braun quickly became a global player in the design world. By the 1960s, trips to Gillette in Boston, to conferences and lectures in the USA, Canada, Mexico, India, Japan and even Cuba were part of Rams's day-to-day. Japan in particular, with its corporate partners and deep-rooted culture, revealed new horizons and experiences to him. People are undoubtedly shaped by their surroundings, and Rams was influenced by his many international contacts and friendships, for example with his kindred spirit, Kenji Ekuan (1929–2015), Japan's most important industrial designer at the time.

Rams is not the 'godfather of design', as he is often called in Asia, but he certainly stood out as more than just one of fifteen Braun designers. As I see it, along with German architect and designer Peter Behrens (1868–1940), Rams was the country's most important, and above all most influential, industrial designer in the twentieth century. The term 'industry' is necessary to emphasize here as it relates specifically to objects for everyday use. Rams is 'the designer's designer', as Sophie Lovell, author of *Dieter Rams: As Little Design as Possible* (2011), once rightly described him. However, the fact that Rams's team at Braun played a significant role in his development, as well as that of the company, cannot be ignored. His interns and temporary employees also deserve to be mentioned, most of whom were graduates from his time teaching at the Hochschule für bildende Künste (University of Fine Arts), Hamburg, where he held a professorship for industrial design from 1981 to 1997. Rams himself has repeatedly emphasized the importance of teamwork in the design process.

THE DESIGNER'S SELF-IMAGE

Dieter Rams, who was born in Wiesbaden in 1932, could never be accused of promoting the salesman-like values of cheap production. He always started from the aesthetic quality of an object, its visual and three-dimensional characteristics, and understood the importance of producing designs with creative longevity. This may have had its roots in his oft-mentioned admiration for his grandfather, a master carpenter who specialized in hand polishing furniture. Or in one of his teachers at the Werkkunstschule (School of Applied Arts) Wiesbaden, director Hans Soeder (1891–1962), who, as a former member of the architectural collective Der Ring,[2] introduced Rams to the principles of the 1920s German Modernist movement and called for the design industry to adopt a social-ethical code of responsibility. The brief time Rams spent in the Frankfurt-based architectural offices of Otto Apel (1906–1966) may also have had an influence, as it was here that he collaborated with the American architecture firm Skidmore, Owings & Merrill, which in turn was strongly influenced by the work of Mies van der Rohe (1886–1969). Hence, when he came to Braun in July 1955, Rams was not an unknown quantity merely implementing the guidelines of the Hochschule für Gestaltung (HfG) Ulm, as is sometimes claimed. The twenty-three-year-old already had his own attitude towards design, which was then additionally fostered by his contacts at the HfG Ulm; his approach was compatible with Ulm, as it were.

In about 1980, after twenty-five years as an industrial designer, Rams expressed his self-image as follows:

> Designers, as I understand them, are critics of civilization, critics of technology, critics of society. But in contrast to the many critical minds that exist today, some with a calling, some without, they must not stop at criticism. They have to keep trying to create something

new that emerges from the criticism and withstands criticism. [...] A shaver or a chair, a film camera or a shelf should have the objective usefulness of tools in their construction and design. They should help people to solve small or large problems. They should help them to be creative themselves. They should live with them and enable them to become friends. [...] As a designer, if you don't close your eyes, you won't be able to stop brooding.[3]

In addition to the critical positivist approach, it is noteworthy that Rams also addresses the emotional connection to products here, which post-modern critics at the time had accused him of lacking. In this same 1980 speech, Rams also refers to the comprehensive approach to design, to the impact of spaces and things on people, to a nature destroyed by ever-increasing consumer waste and to the blatant injustice of superfluous things in rich countries and poverty in developing countries.

BRAUN AND VITSŒ

Rams's understanding of design was further developed at Braun; its particular set-up in the mid-1950s formed the basis and the petri dish for how his practice would evolve. Following the untimely death of Max Braun, the company's founder, in 1951, Erwin Braun (1921–1992) took over the commercial operation of the business, while his brother, Artur (1925–2013), was responsible for the technical and engineering department. Erwin was fundamentally committed to creating a new corporate culture. This culture included a new social understanding of employee well-being and participation, from health services to a company nursery school and employee bonuses. But it also included a new understanding of the product, which was not intended to be impressive, but rather natural and restrained. Braun's advertising campaign called it 'in the style of our time'. This pursuit for a 'contemporary

form' for a new society and for *der Neue Mensch* (the new individual) was clearly a reflection of the design discourse that had dominated the last century, starting with the Arts and Crafts and Art Nouveau movements of the late 1900s, and continuing with the Modernist movement of the early twentieth century.

To help realize this vision, Braun found external designers: first Wilhelm Wagenfeld (1900–1990) in 1954, and then Herbert Hirche (1910–2002) in 1956, although neither was successful in implementing a truly radical new approach. Braun's partnership with the HfG Ulm – fronted by Otl Aicher (1922–1991), the school's co-founder, and Hans Gugelot (1920–1965), one of its lecturers – was initially the most important contributor to the company's design revolution beginning in early 1955. But the geographical distance between Ulm and Frankfurt posed a problem. The Ulm-based designers only visited Frankfurt every two or so months to present their designs to the company's board of directors, and there was very little communication with Braun's technicians and engineers, resulting in a situation that hindered innovation. Erwin and Artur, together with design officer Fritz Eichler (1911–1991), soon realized that the company needed an internal design department. This led to the building of the small team around Rams, with Ulm transitioning to more of an advisory body.[4]

Ultimately, new design could not be achieved at a design college that withdrew into a cloistered atmosphere, as Ulm did. It had to engage with the real world, and Frankfurt was not the worst place for this to happen. Following Germany's Modernist movement of the 1920s, within which architect Ernst May's 'New Frankfurt' housing and design programme was of particular importance to the city, the Nazi regime caused catastrophic devastation and led to an exodus of progressive designers. However, Frankfurt managed to salvage the thriving jazz scene that had boomed

in the pre-war period. Almost all of the American jazz greats performed in the city's Festhalle, followed by jam sessions in the Jazz Keller, to which Rams and others were regular visitors. In terms of atmosphere, jazz formed an important backdrop to the lives and values of Braun's forward-looking team, symbolizing the beginning of a new era. American bebop meanwhile brought a new attitude towards life.

As a result of Braun's new design approach, clever business policy, new marketing strategies, technical innovations, successful acquisitions and foreign subsidiaries, it prospered enormously following the passing of Max Braun in 1951 until its sale to Gillette in 1967. During this period, the total annual turnover increased from 14 to 276 million deutschmarks, and the workforce from 800 to 5,700.[5] In 1962, Braun took over Spanish household appliance manufacturer Pimer (Pequeñas Industrias Mecánico-Eléctricas Reunidas) and, under the name Braun Española, supplied the Spanish market with appliances, some of which were specially designed for the country. However, the design process was still managed by the Germany-based team.

But regarding who ultimately decided what was produced and what was not, Rams described his experiences in a lecture in 1977:

> Who decides about designs? [...] It is unrealistic to expect a company to leave the decision to the designer alone. [...] It would also be unfair to saddle the designer with a decision that affects the entire company. [...] The company's management must be able to rely on the professional expertise of its employees – the engineers, the sales staff and the designers! It cannot reduce any of these three to mere lackeys. [...] And yet they cannot allow the specialists to make the decisions alone. From my point of view, the reality is that the designers prepare the decision to a large

extent, and greatly limit the possible leeway in the decision-making. […] Management cannot go to the drawing board or create models themselves. They can only accept, influence and reject. I honestly have to say that many a good design has fallen by the wayside […] But I also have to say that I basically do not consider any other solution to be sensible or realistic. It is good when decisions about design are made at the highest level in a qualified and competent manner – good for the company, good for the designers.[6]

Over the years, Rams developed a strategy of presenting only fully developed prototypes to the decision-making committees. He deliberately refrained from giving interim presentations to avoid raising concern over half-finished products, which would then cling to the finished designs as well.

Rams's work for Vitsœ began almost simultaneously with his work for Braun. He was initially hired by Braun in July 1955 as an interior designer, so was mainly involved with furnishing the offices and guest flats of the company's Rüsselsheimer Straße headquarters; his sketch of a showroom dating from 1955 has been preserved (pp. 20–1). During the same period, he also designed furniture for his own apartment and that of his colleague Marlene Schneyder (p. 26). In early 1956, he met Otto Zapf (1931–2018), the son of a cabinetmaker and furniture dealer in Eschborn, not far from Frankfurt. At the time, Zapf was a physics student at the Goethe-Universität Frankfurt, but he also had experience with furniture making, having collaborated on some projects with the architect Rolf Schmidt (1930–). After initially hesitating to take over his father's company, Zapf founded RZ-Möbelvertriebs in 1956, with the intention of producing Rams's designs, as well as those of others. The RZ 57 furniture series (pp. 27–9) was developed as part of this early partnership. The RZ 57 was a modular

system which allowed a number of different furniture items, including tables, beds, shelving and cabinets, to be freely assembled by the user and also to be combined with one another to create integrated units. However, due to the limited capacity of Zapf's carpentry workshop, manufacture of the system initially proved challenging. This soon changed when Danish furniture dealer Niels Vitsoe (1913–1995) joined the company in 1958, and promptly expanded its capacity to both produce and sell its products. It was renamed Vitsoe+Zapf on 1 May 1961. Through Vitsoe's contacts, he found a partner in nearby Kelkheim, namely the Richter furniture factory, which could take on the production of the RZ 57. The fact that, at twenty-four years old, Rams was committed to taking on this opportunity and the added responsibility is quite remarkable, especially since his work at Braun was becoming more and more time-consuming. However, it allowed him a level of mental and material independence that would ultimately be beneficial for both companies.

The design process at Vitsoe+Zapf was more personal and direct than at Braun. No presentation prototypes were required; instead, businessman Niels Vitsoe was always available as a sounding board. It was a design process among friends, which often involved Rams's wife as well, the photographer Ingeborg Kracht-Rams. Rams's design approach, however, stayed true to his method at Braun: designing things that are functional, aesthetic, understated, and technically and visually enduring. His 606 Universal Shelving System (pp. 65–9) is the perfect example of this consistency and conviction. It has been in continuous production since 1960, with numerous updates and additions being made throughout the years, but the underlying principle is that all new modifications must be compatible with the existing system. The 606 is currently manufactured and distributed worldwide by Mark Adams, managing director of Vitsoe's

UK-based operation, who, after successfully marketing Vitsoe products in the UK since 1985, took over production of the system in 1995, following Niels Vitsoe's retirement.

On 17 October 1969, Otto Zapf left the partnership, pursuing a career as a furniture designer in the United States, primarily for Knoll International. Thus Vitsoe+Zapf became simply Vitsoe, and the now solo operation required a new look. The task fell to graphic designer Wolfgang Schmidt (1929–1995), who was instrumental in defining the company's corporate identity for more than twenty years; in 1970, he combined the o and e in the company logo to form the œ in the name Vitsœ, reminiscent of the French word *œuvre*, meaning a work of art. Numerous other graphics by Schmidt have been revived by Vitsœ in recent years, and they still fit the brand perfectly.

DESIGN AND TECHNIQUE

Since Rams has always based his designs on functionality, intensive cooperation with engineers was an integral part of his practice, and he was often involved in the technical development of products. Numerous patents and utility model applications submitted by Braun in his name attest to this.[7] One of the earliest was filed in 1959 for Rams's LE 1 loudspeakers (p. 55); another followed in 1968 for the T 2 cylindric table lighter (p. 149), although this was preceded by one for the design of its storage case, which doubled as an ashtray and cigarette box. However, the case would not make its debut until 1974, when Braun created the prototypes for the solar-powered 'energetic' lighter (pp. 208–9).

Rams is credited as the lead inventor of the patented F1 mactron pocket lighter design from 1971 (p. 184), having created the novel opening mechanism, which allows the user to single-handedly flip open the ignition and light the flame. In 1972, the HLD 4 hair dryer (pp. 172–3) with its innovative blower construction, received a patent in Japan and the USA. A year later, on 31 January 1973, the distinctive tuning dial on Rams's audio 308 compact sound system (p. 201), which featured two finger recesses, was registered for a patent; with one finger you can quickly turn through the whole tuning scale, while the second recess allows for fine tuning. The raised dial sits flush with the housing of the tuner and operation is automatically halted with the release of the finger.

In 1979, a patent was issued for Rams's design of a car loudspeaker, the L 100 auto (p. 223), which had a frame made of shock-absorbent material to prevent injuries. He received another in 1980 for a mounting mechanism used on the loudspeaker grilles for Braun's atelier sound system (p. 283). In 1984, Rams was issued his first patent for Gillette with the design of a gas-powered torch (p. 290). However, his greatest economic success for the American company was undoubtedly the Sensor razor (pp. 318–19), for which he and Jürgen Greubel designed the handle in 1989 – and which went on to sell more than one hundred million units.

The final example worth mentioning is an older patent from 1969, which was registered in the USSR, for the (as yet unknown) design of an electric toothbrush (p. 154). The mention of the country is just as surprising as the year, because with the exception of the pioneering Mayadent model from 1963, Braun's production of electric toothbrushes did not begin until 1978.

In contrast to technical inventions, the legal protection of entire designs was different. Braun usually only registered its own company designs for protection. Rams, however, was granted a very rare recognition concerning his 620 chair programme for Vitsœ (pp. 94–5). Following a six-year legal dispute with the company fg Design, which had copied and built the furniture system without a licence, the design was granted an artistic copyright by Germany's highest court,

the Bundesgerichtshof, in 1973. According to the case law at the time, this was a circumstance to which only a handful of design products could lay claim.[8]

PERIODS OF DESIGN

Most of Rams's designs for Braun were created one to two years before the products were released to the market. However, as only a handful of precise development times can be reconstructed from existing archives, this book always indicates the date that sales began. The development of the SK 4 (p. 25), for example, took just nine months until production; the FA 3 film camera (p. 114), likewise, took less than a year. Gerd A Müller's design work on the KM 3 food processor (p. 35) began in December 1955, and its release was in April 1957. For the F1 mactron pocket lighter, we must assume at least three, if not four, years were required for its development due to its complicated construction. Conversely, the typography for the ST 1 credit card-sized calculator from 1987 (p. 310) was designed by Dietrich Lubs in a hotel room in a single day.

THE FOUR PHASES OF DIETER RAMS'S WORK

In looking at Rams's more than sixty-year career, it is possible to identify four distinct phases:

The first phase starts in 1953, after his graduation from the Werkkunstschule Wiesbaden, when he worked at the architectural practice of Otto Apel until 1955, shortly before Braun's design department was formally established. These were Rams's training and apprentice years, during which time his design approach was defined and put into practice. His work on the SK 4 in 1956, as well as on the studio 2 modular hi-fi system (p. 53), TP 1 portable radio and record player (p. 52) and LE 1 loudspeaker, all of which were released in 1959, undoubtedly had a special significance. At the same time, he created the RZ 57 modular furniture system,

which was equally consequential to his development, and laid the foundations for what would become a defining feature of his practice.

The second phase from 1959 to around 1975 represents an extensive period of productivity for Rams, both at Braun and at Vitsœ. Even a quick glance at the products in this catalogue of works demonstrates Rams's impressive output during these years.

The third phase from 1975 to 1997, after he left Braun, was focused on intensive lecturing, teaching at the Hochschule für bildende Künste, Hamburg, serving as president of the German Design Council, participating in juries, collaborative designs with Jürgen Greubel and Dietrich Lubs, and a number of external commissions.

In the fourth phase from 1997 until today, Rams worked for Cologne-based furniture company sdr+ (until 2012) and is, at the time of writing, still working for Vitsœ. In addition, he has participated in numerous interviews, lectures and exhibitions, and produced a number of essays, theoretical texts and publications.

DESIGN CHARACTERISTICS

One question that cannot be answered with a simple 'yes' or 'no' is whether Rams has a definitive design style. In 1977, Rams described his approach to design as follows: 'First of all, we tried – and continue to do so – to understand anew and better what kind of devices people really need, and then what they should look like. And we constantly asked ourselves and others: does it have to be like this?'[9]

For him, having an attitude towards design has always been more important than a style, one that is user-oriented, sensible, ethical and aesthetic. He stated this in his 'ten principles for good design', a set of recommendations that he began to formulate in the 1970s in order to assess what, in his opinion, constituted good design, and which still resonate with young designers today. Also important to mention here is his credo 'less, but better', a motto for change – and potentially the key to a better existence for everyone and for the environment.

Yet there are also formal criteria that can be observed in his products. As a latent architect, Rams often worked with right angles, with cube and rectangular box shapes. A closer look, however, shows that these basic shapes have often been altered in detail: for example, in the slight curvature in the grille of the LE 1 loudspeaker, in the asymmetrically rounded edges of the domino table lighter (p. 225), or in his use of colour to add an element of contrast to his otherwise understated designs. If Rams shows technology, it is technology that has been civilized by design.

Another trait is that his objects are always designed from every angle, even the rear sides that might normally be concealed. He applied this principle as early as 1957, with the RZ 57 modular system, which could be assembled as a free-standing unit and placed anywhere in a room. This holistic approach permeates his entire design practice.

Another central element in Rams's design work is the principle of modularity, or in other words, connectivity. His 606 Universal Shelving System, 620 chair programme and RZ 57 series are flexible systems that can be end-lessly reconfigured, extended and adapted over time according to the needs of the user. From the late 1950s, his audio systems for Braun were also modular and could be combined in multiple ways. What makes the approach so successful is that the different components do not look like autonomous elements casually strung together; instead they produce a considered and harmonious overall form.

Colour also played an important, albeit discreet, role for Rams. His electronic devices were not just black, white or grey, as some critics claimed during the post-modern era. Rams used colours as indicators of operability, but even more important was their ability to bring aesthetic value. He used colour very sparingly, but it was precisely for this reason that it had such an impact. The complementary contrast between red and green played a role again and again, but often Rams opted for a simple red dot. There is virtually no Braun device that he was involved with that goes without this minimalist colour scheme.

Similarly, his use of typography on the devices was very light and restrained, and this would become typical of the Braun style; even on his earliest designs, Rams kept the lettering and the logo very small. However, Dietrich Lubs must also be mentioned in this regard, as he became responsible for the labelling of all devices soon after joining the design department. His consistent use of the Akzidenz-Grotesk font enhanced the longevity of Braun's corporate design.

The final characteristic that was central to Rams's approach, as well as to Braun's, was intuitive user interaction, and it can be traced back to Herbert Hirche's HF 1 television set from 1958, which had only one visible power button. Subsequently, Braun devices came to be defined by the fact that they required no operating instructions; in other words, they were self-explanatory. This was truly a great challenge and achievement, and has been an inspiration for Apple in particular since the early 2000s. For Rams, the objects of our everyday are, and have always been, special; they are the things that deserve our attention, that are in need of improvement and, if possible, reduction. For him, design is not something to be exalted and distinguished, as we are led to believe in a world of consumerism. 'Back to purity, back to simplicity!' is

the last statement of his ten prin-ciples. A motto for new beginnings.

ACKNOWLEDGEMENTS

The best way to approach a designer is through his work, and therefore, this subject was extensively discussed with Dieter Rams, as well as his friends and colleagues, for this book project. *Dieter Rams: The Complete Works* is intended as a source of inspiration for design historians, collectors, designers, students and anyone else who may be interested. For this opportunity, I would first and foremost like to thank Dieter Rams, who was willing to provide access not only to all available documents, but also, through many discussions, and across many years, to his memories as well. I would also like to thank Dieter's wife Ingeborg Kracht-Rams, who contributed photographs from her work at Braun, and his manager Britte Siepenkothen, who, as a long-time confidante, provided many important details and strong support for the project from the beginning. The Dieter und Ingeborg Rams Stiftung (Dieter and Ingeborg Rams Foundation) has provided not only the necessary material through its archive, but also financial support for this book.

Also deserving of a mention here are the key figures of collectors' magazine *Design+Design*, namely Jo Klatt as editor-in-chief and author, plus authors Günter Staeffler and Hartmut Jatzke-Wigand. Over many years, they have published extensive research on the designs of Dieter Rams, the results of which have been incorporated here, and have been very cooperative in every respect for the purposes of this project. With great commitment, photographer Andreas Kugel re-photographed the majority of the objects presented in the book, helping to display them in a suitable light.

Special thanks are also due to Thomas Guttandin, managing

director of the Freunde der BraunSammlung (Friends of the Braun Collection) and head of the Braun Archive, for his wealth of information and suggestions, and to his predecessor Horst Kaupp, who was responsible for building up this significant collection since the 1950s. Thanks also to Petra Stoffel, head of global communications at Braun in Geneva, who has very generously granted the rights to reproduce the archival material in this book. I would also like to warmly thank Julia Schulz of the Vitsœ Archive in Royal Leamington Spa, and Mark Adams, managing director of Vitsœ, for their contributions.

Thanks to Dr Marlene Schnelle-Schneyder, who kindly provided detailed information on the first years of the design revolution at Braun. In addition, I was able to conduct a detailed interview with Artur Braun (1925–2013) in July 2010; over the years, members of the Braun design team have also made themselves available for interviews. I would also like to thank the research assistant of the Rams Archives, Hehn-Chu Ahn, for her support, many an archive discovery and numerous good conversations, as well as the director of the Museum Angewandte Kunst (Museum of Applied Arts), Frankfurt am Main, Professor Matthias Wagner K, for his generous support of my scientific work on Rams at the museum.

But what is the use of all the work if it is not published? A renowned book publisher is always the best medium for this. Publisher at Phaidon Press in London, Emilia Terragni, provided the impetus for this book project and supported it throughout; Robyn Taylor executed it perfectly with very efficient project management, but above all through meticulous editing. In this way, the book was spared many inaccuracies and mistakes, for which I would like to express my special thanks. Finally, designers Jesse Reed and Juan Aranda of Order in New York put it into just the right form.

[1] Jo Klatt and Günter Staeffler, *Braun+Design Collection: 40 Jahre Braun Design – 1955 bis 1995* (*Braun+Design Collection: 40 Years of Braun Design – 1955 to 1995*), 2nd ed (Hamburg, 1995).

[2] Der Ring (1924–1933) was an architectural collective of leading architects from the New Objectivity movement in the Weimar Republic. Some additional members were Peter Behrens, Walter Gropius, Ludwig Mies van der Rohe, Hans Poelzig and Bruno Taut.

[3] Dieter Rams, 'Industriedesign in einer Zeit des Umbruchs' ('Industrial Design at a Time of Change'), lecture held in c.1980, Rams Archive, Frankfurt am Main, 1.1.2.17.

[4] 'And when the food processor was developed here, it was basically already clear that we had to shift our cooperation with Ulm more towards consulting and not direct practical collaboration.' Artur Braun in an interview with the author on 23 July 2010 in Königstein, Germany.

[5] Hans Wichmann, *Mut zum Aufbruch: Erwin Braun 1921–1992* (*Courage to Make a New Start: Erwin Braun 1921–1992*) (Munich, 1998), 140.

[6] Dieter Rams, 'Design ist eine verantwortliche Aufgabe der Industrie' ('Design is a Serious Duty of Industry'), lecture held on 18 February 1977, Rams Archive, Frankfurt am Main, 1.1.2.8.

[7] A binder with originals and copies of such patents is included in the papers of Dieter Rams in the Rams Archive, Frankfurt am Main.

[8] Such as Mart Stam's cantilever chair from 1926 or the USM Haller Modular Furniture System by Fritz Haller from 1963. Under German law, upon the death of the creator, the heirs are entitled to the legal rights for an additional seventy years.

[9] Rams, 'Design ist eine verantwortliche Aufgabe der Industrie'

1947–1959

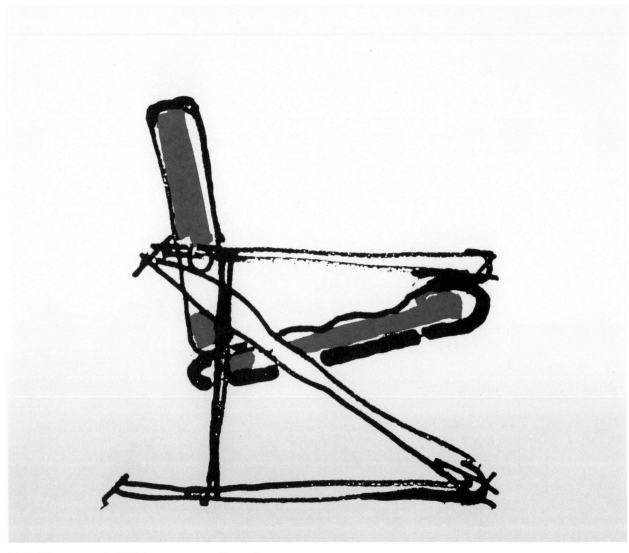

Sketch for an armchair, 1947
Dieter Rams

Size unknown
Black and red marker on paper

The earliest surviving work by Dieter
Rams is this design for an armchair,
which he made while studying at the
Werkkunstschule (School of Applied
Arts) in Wiesbaden, West Germany.
Its reference to modern design of the
1920s is unmistakable; the Z-shaped
framework connecting armrests and
skid base is reminiscent of the cantilever chairs designed by Rams's
contemporaries Mart Stam and
Marcel Breuer. Although the armchair
is without back legs, a thin, vertical
support was added for stability. The
work shows that pre-war Modernism
was remarkably prevalent at the
Wiesbaden school in the 1950s. This
1970s sketch is a facsimile reproduced
from a technical drawing made in 1947.

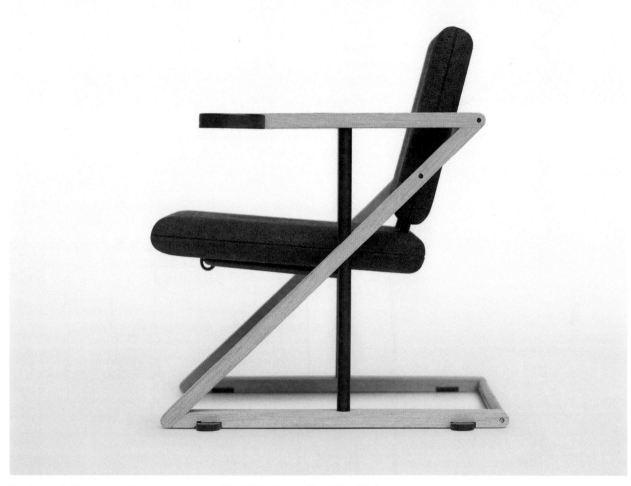

Scale model for an armchair
(reconstruction), c.1952
Dieter Rams

15 × 13.5 × 13 cm (6 × 5¼ × 5 in)
0.04 kg (1½ oz)
Wood

This scale model of the armchair
was later reconstructed from the
sketch under Rams's supervision.

1955 ʍɫ

Sketch for Braun's Rüsselsheimer
Straße showroom, Frankfurt, 1955
Dieter Rams
Braun

29 × 36.8 cm (11½ × 14½ in)

Ink and coloured pencils on paper

One of Rams's first assignments at
Braun was to design a showroom.
This sketch shows it furnished with
Knoll International products, and
featuring the PK-G radio and record
player console designed by Hans
Gugelot for Braun in 1955. In the
background is a shelving system
resembling the RZ 60 that Rams later
designed for Vitsoe+Zapf (pp. 65–9).
Although the showroom was never
realized, its expanse of floor-to-ceiling
glass and bare walls exemplify an
'uncluttered' design approach that
could already be discerned at this
early stage in Rams's career.

exporter 2, 1956
Portable radio
Dieter Rams, HfG Ulm, Charly Ruch
Braun

12 × 17.5 × 5.5 cm (4¾ × 7 × 2 in)
0.9 kg (2 lb)

Plastic
DM 79.50

This portable vacuum tube receiver was a reworking of a Braun factory design for which only the colour scheme, typographic design and transmitter wheel were changed by Rams, in collaboration with designers at the HfG Ulm. The actual casing remained identical, so that no new tooling costs were incurred. Charly Ruch, Braun's graphic designer, updated the scale legend. 'I walked across the yard to the paint shop and all the gold was gone [from the radio],' Rams later recalled about the dramatic transformation. The Braun brothers were amazed at how a small intervention could produce such a huge aesthetic difference.

PA 1, 1956
Automatic slide projector
Dieter Rams
Braun

21.3 × 25 × 18.5 cm (8½ × 10 × 7¼ in)
4.2 kg (9¼ lb)

Die-cast aluminium, plastic
DM 198

The PA 1 slide projector was the first device designed entirely by Rams for Braun, and led to the creation of a new product range for the company. The solid die-cast casing with textured finish stood out from the Prado projectors being produced by market leader Leitz at the time, as well as those of other manufacturers. The PA 1's reduced colour scheme consisted of grey, black and chrome, with the control buttons highly visible in signal red. Even with this refined palette, the device retained an industrial aesthetic. The slides were loaded automatically from the magazine, and could also be operated by remote control. Braun developed a proprietary slide tray system to accompany the product series. However, Leitz's system became the industry standard.

Also in the series: PA 2 (1957)

SK 4, 1956
Prototype for a mono radio-phono
combination
Dieter Rams, Gerd A Müller

Braun
Size and weight unknown

Wood, metal
Not released for sale

This photo of an SK 4 prototype
from the Braun Archive in Kronberg,
Germany, illustrates the design's early
development, as guided by Rams,
and with the assistance of Gerd
A Müller. Its light rectangular box
design was created first in a taller
version (pictured), then a shorter and
wider one, corresponding to the final
proportions. The placement and
number of horizontal slots seen on the
front of the prototype, as well as the
arrangement of the controls, match
those found on the mass-produced
device. For acoustic purposes, Braun
technicians initially gave the SK 4 a
wooden framework, which was then
reinforced with metal panelling. This
represented a new approach in

German radio design, as all-wood or
all-plastic enclosures had been used
almost exclusively until that time.
However, the metal was attached
at a slight distance from the body,
producing horizontal and vertical
gaps around the edges of the unit –
a less than satisfactory visual solution.
In response, designer Hans Gugelot
suggested using metal more
consistently, dispensing with the main
wooden framework. The result was
a four-fold sheet of metal braced
between two wooden side panels,
inside of which all the components of
the device were housed. Although its
assembly was much more complex
than it appeared, the new design was
far more convincing.

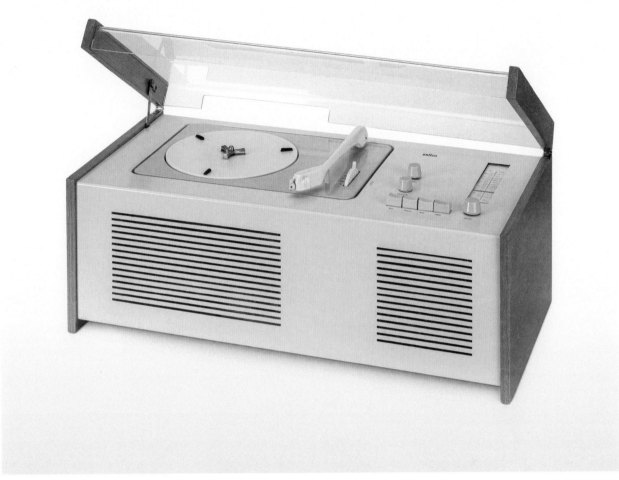

SK 4, 1956
Mono radio-phono combination
Dieter Rams, Hans Gugelot,
Gerd A Müller, Werkstatt Wagenfeld:

Ralph Michel, Helmut Warneke,
Heinz G Pfaender
Braun
24 × 58.4 × 29.4 cm (9½ x 23 x 11½ in)

11.5 kg (25½ lb)
Lacquered sheet steel, elm, acrylic,
plastic
DM 295

The SK 4 is considered a major turning point in Braun design. Work began on the sound system – also known as 'Snow White's Coffin' due to its distinctive acrylic dust cover – at the end of 1955, following an instruction from Erwin and Artur Braun. Rams designed the original framework and basic layout of the phonograph and controls, and the tonearm was designed by Gerd A Müller. The three-speed record player – based on a design from Werkstatt Wagenfeld, an external studio run by Wilhelm Wagenfeld – would later be released separately as the PC 3 (p. 30). For the enclosure, Hans Gugelot, who led the product design programme at the HfG Ulm, swapped Rams's original metal-

veneered wooden body for a full metal casing with wooden sides. The transparent acrylic cover was added by Braun (Rams in collaboration with the head of special purchases, Hagen Gross) and was manufactured by Opelit Bootswerft & Kunststoff-Gesellschaft, a company in Offenbach which had previously supplied acrylic advertising displays for Braun. The SK 4/1 model from 1957 was updated with a four-speed record player.

Sales of the SK 4 were initially sluggish, and there was limited acceptance of the product among radio dealers. However, this all changed with the 1957 Interbau (International Building) exhibition, where more than sixty

Braun radio and television sets were presented in model apartments. Subsequently, several Braun products won awards at the Milan Triennial in July 1957, for which the company garnered significant media coverage. The inclusion of Braun products at Expo 58 in Brussels and in the exhibition *20th Century Design from the Museum Collection,* at the Museum of Modern Art, New York, in 1958–9, resulted in an even greater international profile – and a huge increase in sales, with approximately 16,000 units produced.

Also in the series: SK 4/1 and SK 4/1a (1957), SK 4/2 (1958)

25

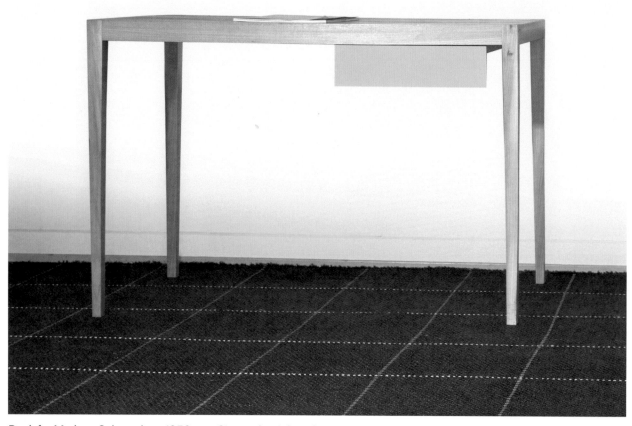

Desk for Marlene Schneyder, c.1956
Dieter Rams
Marlene Schneyder

Size and weight unknown

Light elm, white lacquer
Not released for sale

Alongside Rams's work on the interior
of Braun's Rüsselsheimer Straße
factory showroom in 1955 (pp. 20–1),
he also undertook personal furniture
design projects, including the furn-
ishings for his own apartment and that
of his colleague Marlene Schneyder.
This one-of-a-kind table with slender
legs forms part of this series of
early works.

569 rectangular (RZ 57), 1956–7
Table programme
Dieter Rams
Vitsoe+Zapf / Vitsœ / sdr+

Various sizes and weights

Laminated wood, anodized and
brushed aluminium
DM 596–660 (prices from 1973)

Modular furniture first became available in the 1920s, following key early works by the architects Walter Gropius at the Bauhaus in Weimar, Germany, and Frankfurt-based Franz Schuster. Building on this heritage, Hans Gugelot designed the M 125 furniture system for Wohnbedarf AG in Zurich in 1950, and Rams soon embarked on his own modular projects, the first of which was a table/desk for the small Eschborn-based company Zapf (soon to be Vitsoe+Zapf).

The table's surface was formed of two laminated wood panels, which were set apart to create a narrow shelf in between. The double layer also provided greater stability as it allowed the table legs to be affixed at two separate points. Rams's use of visible black screws is a nod to the design's assembly and adds to its functional aesthetic. The 569 and 570 desks were the first element of what would become an expanded modular range, the RZ 57.

Rams was first introduced to Zapf through Otto Zapf, the son of its founder, who sought out Rams's talents in a bid to expand his father's business. This fortuitous meeting led to the founding of Vitsoe+Zapf (a collaboration between Otto Zapf and Danish furniture salesman Niels Vitsoe), which was set up in 1959 solely to produce and distribute Rams's designs. Also present in these early stages were architect Rolf Schmidt and graphic designer Günther Kieser, also collaborators of Zapf's. The tightknit group was united by a keen interest in contemporary jazz.

Also in the series: 570 rounded (1956–7)

571 / 572 (RZ 57), 1957
Modular furniture assembly system
Dieter Rams
Vitsoe+Zapf

44–205 × 57/114 cm (17¼–80¾ ×
22½/45 in)
Various weights

Lacquered blockboard with resin
or natural beech veneer, laminated
hardboard, anodized aluminium, plastic
DM 18–138

Otto Zapf first met the Danish furniture dealer Niels Vitsoe at the Cologne Furniture Fair in 1957. Two years later they founded the company Vitsoe+Zapf to produce and market the furniture designed by Rams; the RZ 57 modular system was the company's first product range. The system allows the creation of complex and variable cabinet-and-shelf combinations, which can be adapted or extended as needed. It consists of wooden panels and invisible perforated metal strips as connectors. The front and back of each unit were designed to mirror each other, enabling the assembled furniture to stand freely in a room. Rams described the numerous possibilities for application: 'Living room furniture, sideboards, half-height cupboards, shelves, escritoires with a screwed-in writing surface, bedroom furniture, children's furniture, wardrobes, under-bed storage drawers, combined room and office furniture, filing cabinets, work surfaces, shelves with or without doors'. The bay widths of 57 cm (22½ in) and 114 cm (45 in) also enabled the seamless installation of Braun hi-fi sound systems and loudspeakers. Mass production began in 1959.

Following Otto Zapf's departure from the company in 1969, his name was removed from the brand and the graphic designer Wolfgang Schmidt made a small typographic change to the remaining 'Vitsoe' to create the Vitsœ logo we recognize today. This adjustment drew on the French word œuvre, meaning a work of art.

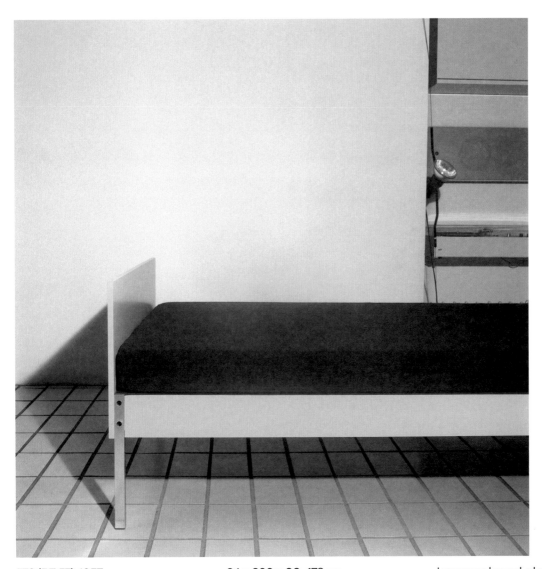

573 (RZ 57), 1957
Bed programme
Dieter Rams
Vitsoe+Zapf

34 × 200 × 90–173 cm
(13½ × 78¾ × 35½–68 in)
Various weights

Lacquered wood, aluminium
DM 298–488 (prices from 1973)

As part of the RZ 57 furniture series, the 573 bed programme contained the same elements as Rams's two-panel 569 and 570 desks (p. 27), but it allowed different types of composition. The attachment of the bed's legs to the two layers of the frame provided stability and the visible black screws formed a key element of its appearance.

PC 3, 1956
Record player
Dieter Rams, Gerd A Müller, Werkstatt
Wagenfeld: Ralph Michel, Helmut

Warneke, Heinz G Pfaender
Braun
13 × 30.8 × 21 cm (5 × 12 × 8¼ in)
2.5 kg (5½ lb)

Metal, plastic
DM 78 (PC 3 SV)

This small record player formed part
of the SK 4 radio-phonograph (p. 25)
but was later also sold as a separate
unit. Developed between February
and September 1956, it was originally
designed at Werkstatt Wagenfeld in
Stuttgart, but the studio was unable
to find a satisfying form. Certain parts
of the design were moved to the
Braun factory in Frankfurt, where the
chassis was straightened and the
tonearm reworked. The design of the
platter remained in Stuttgart where its
distinctive rubber nubs and retractable
central star were retained. As with
Rams's initial design for the SK 4, the
PC 3 came with a set of short legs.

Also in the series: PC 3 SV (1959)

Phonokoffer PC 3, 1956
Portable record player
Dieter Rams, Gerd A Müller, Werkstatt
Wagenfeld: Ralph Michel, Helmut

Warneke, Heinz G Pfaender
Braun
13.5 × 33 × 25.7 cm (5¼ × 13 × 10 in)
3.4 kg (7½ lb)

Wood, metal, plastic, rubber, synthetic
fabric upholstery
DM 98

The PC 3 record player (opposite) was
adapted into a portable device that
could be connected to a stationary hi-fi
system or to a portable radio, and was
designed for mains connection rather
than being battery-operated. The
power cable is stowed for transport in
a compartment within the chamfered
front panel. The wood-and-plastic
case is covered with plastic-coated
fabric, some of which was produced by
inmates at Münster prison. At the time,
the device was mainly used at schools
and universities, as well as adult
training courses and seminars.

Also in the series: Phonokoffer PC 3
SV (1959), PCK 4 stereo (1960)

atelier 1, 1957 / atelier 1-81 stereo, 1959
(pictured)
Compact stereo sound system
Dieter Rams

Braun
29.7 × 58.3 × 29 cm (11¾ × 23 × 11½ in)
13 kg (28½ lb)

Lacquered wood, elm, glass
DM 395

With its familiar rectangular shape
and wooden side panels, the atelier 1
stereo sound system has a clear
kinship with the SK 4 (p. 25). However,
its structure is more conventional.
Taking its lead from several of Braun's
combined stereo systems from the
1930s, the record player is positioned
above the radio and the cover is made
of lacquered wood. The tuning scale
and control buttons were taken from
designer Hans Gugelot's first radio
for Braun, the G 11 from 1955.

Also in the series: atelier 1 stereo
(1958–9), atelier 2 (1960–1), atelier 11
stereo (1961)

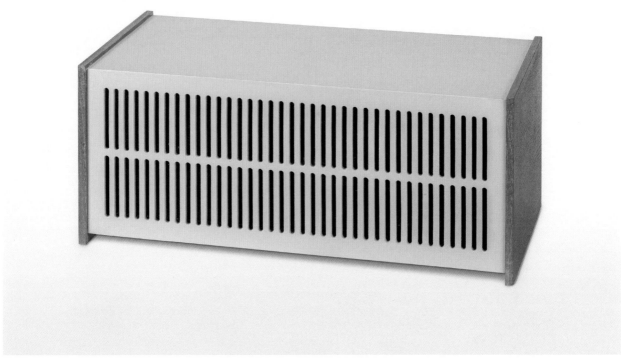

L 1, 1957
Loudspeaker
Dieter Rams
Braun

23.8 × 58.2 × 29 cm (9½ × 23 × 11½ in)
5.3 kg (11¾ lb)

Laminated wood, elm
DM 110

This loudspeaker was developed for the atelier 1 compact device (opposite), which did not come with its own built-in version. To achieve stereophonic reproduction, two loudspeakers had to be positioned a certain distance from each other in the room. The L 1 was also given two-way technology that was sophisticated for the time, where bass/mid-range and treble tones were reproduced by different drivers. Designed to be both visually and technically compatible with other Braun stereo systems, the loudspeaker could be paired with devices ranging from the SK 4 to the SK 55 in order to significantly improve their sound, which was often compromised by their metal construction. The L 1's enclosure, conversely, was made of white laminated wood with elm side panels, resulting in higher quality acoustics.

Also in the series: L 11 (1960), L 12 (1961)

combi DL 5, 1957
Electric shaver
Dieter Rams, Gerd A Müller
Braun

9.5 × 7 × 3.8 cm (3¾ × 2¾ × 1½ in)
0.3 kg (½ lb)

Metal, plastic
DM 58–70

The design of the combi DL 5 shaver provided the shape on which the later, highly successful sixtant model (p. 102) was based. The small, well-rounded, rectangular design fits snugly in the hand and features thin grooves for a better grip. A red or black company logo positioned to one side on a white background is the shaver's only ornament. This small nameplate can also be found on Rams's PA 1 and PA 2 slide projectors (p. 23) and on several other Braun products. The name 'combi' refers to the fact the shaver is combined with a hair trimmer.

KM 3, 1957
Food processor
Gerd A Müller
Braun

26.5 × 37.5 × 24 cm (10½ × 14¾ × 9½ in)
7 kg (15½ lb)

Plastic
DM 198–245

The KM 3 food processor is one of Braun's best-known appliances and was manufactured until the 1990s. Its appearance is the antithesis of the streamlined aesthetics of the American-designed KitchenAid stand mixer, which has been in production since 1936. Artur Braun and the company's engineers developed the first functional prototypes in 1955, but they needed a skilled model-maker to help establish the mixer's final form. Rams recommended Gerd A Müller, a friend he had studied with at Wiesbaden, and who would go on to become a key member of the design team at Braun. Müller joined the project at the end of 1955, quickly developing a more resolved design, free of the modern industrial styling that was prevalent at the time. Rams and Müller shared a workshop at the company throughout 1956.

The KM 3 has a sleek and fluid outline, intersected by horizontal cuts that serve to define its three main elements: motor, gearbox and cantilevered mixing head. Several different attachments could be used in place of the standard mixer. The muted blue of the rotary switch is reflected in the attachment unit: an early example of Braun employing colour to indicate function. A later model, the KM 32 from 1964, which featured an even subtler use of colour and an alternative mixing head design, was developed with the help of Robert Oberheim. Across the KM series, approximately 2.3 million units were produced.

Also in the series: KM 31 (1957), KM 32 and KM 32 B (1964)

transistor 1, 1957 / T 22, 1960 (pictured)
Portable radio
Dieter Rams
Braun

21 × 28.5 × 9.5 cm (8¼ × 11¼ × 3¾ in)
2.5 kg (5½ lb)

Plastic, acrylic
DM 215

The simple rectangular shape of Braun's first portable transistor radio set the standard for the company's later pocket versions, though it was much larger and more powerful. Such early radio devices contained a combination of four vacuum tubes and three transistors, so were not yet fully transistorized. Rams placed the tuning scale on the front, as was the norm on competitors' devices, which was useful for upright operation. Taking aesthetic cues from the SK stereo range and L 1 loudspeaker (p. 33), Rams incorporated horizontal openings for the loudspeaker and tube cooling on the front of the radio. Notably, the designer was mentioned by name in the press release for Braun's product launch – designer acknowledgements were remarkably rare at the time. The transistor 1 was later developed into various other models with different wave ranges.

Also in the series: transistor 2 (1958), transistor k (1959), T 22-C, T 23 and T 24 (1960), T 220 (1961), T 225 (1963)

L 2, 1958
Loudspeaker with skid-legged stand
Dieter Rams
Braun

72 × 43 × 32 cm (28¼ × 17 × 13 in)
16 kg (35¼ lb)

Laminated wood, natural wood, metal,
nickel-plated steel
DM 235

The large L 2 floor-standing loud speaker from 1958 featured a rectangular wooden body set on a double-skid-legged stand made of curved and nickel-plated tubular steel. The black perforated speaker grille on the front of the design is set into a white laminated-wood surface, which also extends to the back side, and the side panels came in walnut or white beech veneer. Reminiscent of, and aesthetically compatible with, Rams's atelier series of sound systems (p. 32), the L 2 successfully combined different materials and colours. The white and black shades form a stark contrast to one another, which perfectly suits the geometric design. Likewise, the wide radius of the tubular steel skids complements the 90-degree angles of the speaker enclosure, while the metallic base acts as a counterpoint to the warm, matt finish of the wood siding. Although it was only produced in a small run of 400 units, to a certain extent, this 'sound furniture' was already heralding the new aesthetics for advanced technology; with the L 2's three built-in loudspeaker drivers, it provided a whole new listening experience.

SK 5, 1958
Mono radio-phono combination
Dieter Rams, Hans Gugelot,
Gerd A Müller, Werkstatt Wagenfeld:
Ralph Michel, Helmut Warneke,
Heinz G Pfaender
Braun

24 × 58.4 × 29.4 cm (9½ × 23 × 11½ in)
11.5 kg (25½ lb)

Metal, plastic, acrylic, elm
DM 325

The SK 5 was the almost identical
successor to the SK 4/2 with the
exception of an additional long-wave
radio band, which required a fifth
push button to operate. Moreover, the
device no longer had to be connected
to an umbrella antenna, but rather a
1-m (3-ft) -long plug-in wire aerial. This
provided greater flexibility in terms of
placement in a room, as it only needed
to be connected to the mains. The
record player also offered four speeds
instead of three. Braun manufactured
between 15,000 and 30,000 units in
total. The SK 5c model for export to the
USA and Canada had a short-wave
receiver instead of long-wave.

Also in the series: SK 5c (1960)

Prototype for a portable record player, 1958
Dieter Rams
Braun

9 × 29.2 × 23.7 cm (3½ × 11½ × 9¼ in)
2.7 kg (6 lb)

Plastic, metal, rubber
Not released for sale

This portable record player, which can also be wall-mounted, was designed to match the radio (opposite). The dust cover was designed with a 90-degree opening mechanism that allows the record player to remain in a horizontal position when in use – which is the only way to make it operate. Another remarkable design feature is the tonearm, which fits flush into the unit when not in use. The intention with these first prototypes was to create an entire wall-mounted system, as proposed by the HfG Ulm.

Prototype for a portable radio, 1958
Dieter Rams
Braun

23 × 16 × 7.2 cm (9 × 6¼ × 2¾ in)
0.5 kg (11 lb)

Plastic, paper, aluminium
Not released for sale

Throughout 1956 and 1957, the number of different ideas for Braun radios was growing, both at the HfG Ulm and at the company's Frankfurt factory. Modularity became a major talking point, with discussions on how could things fit together and also complement each other. Portability was another major consideration, along with the development of new presentation formats. The HfG Ulm began work on a new modular hi-fi sound system project for Braun, which Herbert Lindinger, then a student at the school, later submitted as his diploma. Rams continued this concept and designed matching hi-fi separates, such as those used in the studio 2 sound system (p. 53).

At the same time, he developed a modular concept for this small portable radio and battery-operated record player (opposite). The radio features a tuning scale that runs the entire width of the casing and a round perforated speaker grille. Openings on the back allow it to be mounted on a wall.

T 3, 1958
Pocket radio
Dieter Rams, HfG Ulm
Braun

8.2 × 18.8 × 4 cm (3¼ × 7½ × 1½ in)
0.45 kg (1 lb)

Plastic
DM 120

The advancement of transistor technology in the 1950s made it possible to shrink the size of portable radios, which became known as pocket radios. The first commercial transistor radio, the Regency TR-1, was released to the US market in 1954, and can be seen as early inspiration for the T 3. Another of Rams's influences was the Sony TR-63, which appeared in Japan in 1957 and was the first radio to be described as 'pocket-sized'. The Sony device featured a pronounced tuning dial, elements of which can be seen reflected T 3's dial, originally designed by Otl Aicher and Hans G Conrad at the HfG Ulm. However, their first iteration did not make it into production; Rams's subsequent refinement resulted in a more coherent and visually convincing solution.

The speaker grille consists of 121 circular openings arranged in a square grid and the Braun logo is very discreetly positioned on the back of the device; a light leather case was made to accompany the T 3, on which the logo was much more evident – likely an opportunity seized on by the marketing department. The T 3 is often considered an early inspiration for the Apple iPod (2001–14); its designer, Jonathan Ive, has often spoken of his admiration for Rams.

Also in the series: T 31 (1960)

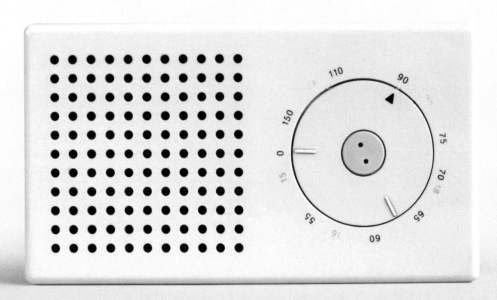

S 60 Standard 1, 1958
Electric shaver
Dieter Rams, Gerd A Müller
Braun

10 × 5.5 × 3.2 cm (4 × 2 × 1¼ in)
0.25 kg (½ lb)

Plastic, metal
DM 35

The designs for Braun shavers evolved gradually over a series of small steps. The S 60 is a slimmer version of the combi DL 5 (p. 34) but without the hair trimmer. This model was easier for those with smaller hands to use and, above all, significantly cheaper.

Also in the series: S 60 Standard 2 (1960), S 62 Standard 3 (1962), S 63 Standard (1965)

MX 3, 1958 / MX 32, 1962 (pictured)
Blender
Gerd A Müller
Braun

40 × 14 cm in diameter (15¾ × 5½ in)
4.5 kg (10 lb)

Plastic
DM 110

This mixer borrowed the design language established with Braun's KM 3 food processor from 1957 (p. 35). Two diverging cone-like segments meet in the middle of the appliance to form a distinct 'waist', which gives the design a visual lightness. The wide metal ring connecting motor unit to glass jug indicates how the top section can be removed; a large rotary switch with a rectangular grip is the only control element.

Also in the series: MX 31 (1958), MX 32 B (1962)

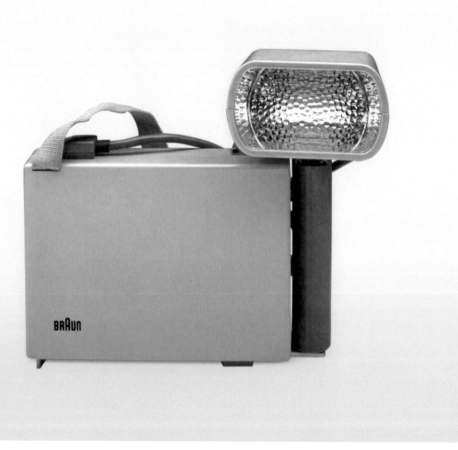

EF 1 hobby standard, 1958
Electronic camera flash
Dieter Rams
Braun

21 × 20 × 10 cm (8¼ × 8 × 4 in)
2.5 kg (5½ lb)

Plastic
DM 185 (EF 2-NC)

In the mid-1950s, camera flashes became a completely new business segment for Braun. The idea was likely conceived during a visit by Erwin Braun and his friend, the physicist Dr Gerhard Lander, to the Photokina photography and imaging trade fair in Cologne in 1952. Braun's intention was to produce a device that was only half the price of those available on the market. After only seven months of development, it became a reality in 1953 with the Hobby de Luxe, costing 198 deutschmarks. However, its design was still based on a 1930s model, so Rams adapted it to fit the company's new design approach. Due to its technical requirements, the EF 1 was a rather hefty device consisting of power unit, batteries and flash head. Rams enclosed the power unit in a thin rectangular box with a completely smooth finish. The black Braun logo positioned in the bottom left helps to visually balance the flash head in the top right, which could also be mounted directly on to a camera. Over time, camera flashes became increasingly smaller; the flashes built into today's smartphones are a striking example of the extreme miniaturization of electronics.

Also in the series: EF 2-NC hobby special (1958)

D 50, 1958
Prototype for an automatic slide
projector with remote control
Dieter Rams

Braun
26.5 × 33.5 × 14 cm (10½ × 13¼ × 5½ in)
6 kg (31¼ lb)

Plastic, metal
Not released for sale

This slide projector was only realized
in a small pre-production run of fifty
devices, but it can be seen as the
starting point for a whole new range
of Braun products. Unlike the PA 1 from
1956 (p. 23), the D 50 was informed by
the simple rectangular shape of the SK
stereo range. There were no more push
buttons; instead, these were replaced
with circular knobs, and all the
technical components were enclosed
in a box-like casing from which only
the projection lens and controls
emerged. The wired remote control
matched the form of the projector and
was given a concave push-button
switch. These decisions demonstrate
how, after only a brief period, Rams
had developed an entirely new attitude

to this type of device, which in turn
would influence later designs such
as the D 40 of 1961 (p. 72).

The design of the D 50 was initiated
by an instruction from Artur Braun,
who wanted to establish a slide tray
system that could become the industry
standard. He assigned a dedicated
engineer to the task, but the technically
sophisticated solution turned out to
be too expensive to succeed in the
market. The D 50's distinctive shape,
the position of the slide magazine
under the lens and the addition of a
rocker switch to change the projector's
vertical inclination were revisited by
Robert Oberheim for the D 300 model
of 1970 (p. 171).

Also in the series: D 45 (1961), D 47
(1966), D 46 and D 46 J (1967)

H 1, 1959
Fan heater
Dieter Rams
Braun

8.5 × 27.5 × 13.5 cm (3¼ × 10½ × 5¼ in)
2 kg (4½ lb)

Metal, plastic
DM 89

This small and powerful fan heater caused a sensation when it was released, both in terms of technology and design. With an output of 2,000 watts and a far-reaching air flow, it could heat both small and larger rooms. Its compact design was made possible by the tangential fan invented by the engineer Bruno Eck and physicist Nikolaus Laing in 1956, which replaced the conventional propeller and was significantly quieter and smaller. Taking advantage of this innovation, Rams designed an equally impressive casing. Two light grey rectangular boxes form the left and right sides; the larger right section holds the motor and gearbox. The middle section is enclosed in a dark

grey housing that contains the fan and heating elements. A slotted air intake grille is located on top and the air outlet is at the front. A swivel foot allows the position of the device to be adjusted. Braun later used the patented fan technology in numerous other devices.

Although this was still early in his career, Rams's design approach is clearly recognizable in the H 1: his use of achromatic colours (white, grey and black); a closed, brick-like silhouette; and the inclusion of a few restrained yet eye-catching design elements. Consequently, the project represented Rams's breakthrough as the most important designer at Braun.

Also in the series: H 11 (1959), H 2 and H 21 (1960)

F 60 hobby (1959) / F 30 b hobby, 1959; F 65 hobby, 1962 (pictured)
Electronic camera flash
Dieter Rams

Braun
19.3 × 11.3 × 5.8 cm (7½ × 4½ × 2¼ in)
0.9 kg (2 lb)

Plastic, metal
DM 178

Compared to the EF 1 hobby standard of 1958 (p. 46), the power unit on this series of electronic flashes required even less space; starting with the F 60, the packaging was reduced to a slim, vertical rectangular box. Gradually modified over a period of ten years, the design's flash head was also reduced in size and adapted to visually reflect the power unit casing.

Also in the series: F 650 hobby (1965), F 655 hobby (1969), F 655 LS hobby-mat (1969)

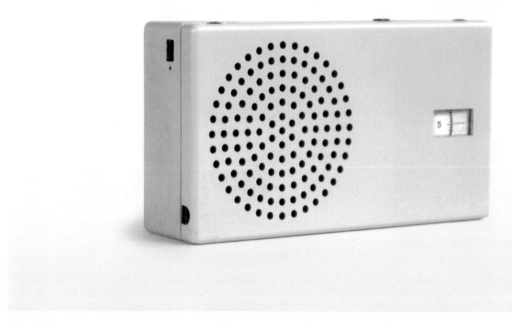

T 4, 1959
Pocket radio
Dieter Rams
Braun

8.2 × 14.8 × 4 cm (3¼ × 5¾ × 1½ in)
0.5 kg (1 lb)

Plastic
DM 135–150

Following on from the T 3 of 1958
(pp. 42–3), this second pocket radio
had a round speaker grille formed
of concentric circle openings and a
tuning scale framed by a small window
of only 10 x 20 mm (approximately
½ × ¾ in); the embedded dial was
numbered from 1 to 7. This was one of
Rams's most minimal design solutions,
and could be considered a radio for
'existentialists'. But there was more to it;
namely, an additional short-wave
receiver. The Braun logo on the back
was even smaller than its predecessor,
at only 8 mm (less than ½ in) wide.
The T 4 pocket radio also came with
a matching leather case manufactured
by a supplier in Offenbach.

P 1, 1959
Portable battery-operated record
player
Dieter Rams

Braun
4 × 14.8 × 14.8 cm (1½ × 5¾ × 5¾ in)
0.6 kg (1¼ lb)

Plastic, metal
DM 59

This portable miniature 7-inch record
player was designed to be combined
with Braun's pocket radio series. The
record is fitted onto a spindle and held
in place by ball bearings. Attached to
a spring-loaded Elac KST 11 crystal
phono cartridge, the stylus is pressed
against the record from the underside
and then disappears into a recess
behind a sliding metal panel when not
in use. The P 1 could be connected to
a pocket radio by cable. Both devices
could also be inserted into an anodized
aluminium carrying case, turning
them into a portable sound system.

TP 1, 1959
Combined radio and record player
Dieter Rams
Braun

23.5 × 15.3 × 4.3 cm (9¼ × 6 × 1¾ in)
1.35 kg (3 lb)

Plastic, metal, rubber, leather
DM 215

Listening to music on the go is largely taken for granted today; many people wear headphones and carry a music device of some kind while travelling through the city. However, the model for today's mini sound systems was not only the Sony Walkman from 1979, but also a set of devices that Rams had designed for Braun twenty years earlier. It combined the newly developed T 4 pocket radio with the P 1 miniature record player (p. 50–1). In terms of design, the device is defined exclusively by rectangles and circles, resulting in a composition that is as exciting as it is harmonious. The combination of light grey plastic casing, the metallic sheen of the record player spindle with its surrounding dark grey rubber ring, and the contrasting red pointer found on the tuning scale of the T 41 radio (p. 87) – a later combination model – has a highly pictorial quality and appears as a collage of precision materials.

Also in the series: TP 2 (1960)

studio 2: CS 11, CE 11, CV 11, 1959
Modular hi-fi system
Dieter Rams
Braun

CS 11: 16.5 × 39.7 × 32.1 cm (6½ × 15½ × 12½ in); CE 11 and CV 11: 10.6 × 19.7 × 32 cm (4¼ × 7¾ × 12½ in)
Various weights

Lacquered sheet steel, aluminium, plastic, acrylic
CS 11: DM 700; CE 11: DM 400; CV 11: DM 350

In 1960, a group of Japanese architects published the manifesto *Metabolism 1960: Proposals for a New Urbanism*. The impetus for this was a growing awareness of Japan's fast-developing cities, for which they did not want to apply a rigid master plan, but rather an adaptable 'planning system' that was better suited to a constantly changing society and offered flexibility of growth. This modular principle had been present in architecture since Karl Friedrich Schinkel's Bauakademie (Building Academy) in Berlin (1831–6), and was later seen in Joseph Paxton's 1851 Crystal Palace in London, as well as in the work of Modernist architects such as Mies van der Rohe, Konrad Wachsmann and Kisho Kurokawa.

In the field of design, Hans Gugelot first applied this modular approach to his early wood designs for Braun in 1955. Four years later, Rams began implementing this same thinking in his consumer electronics, starting with the studio 2 sound system. Building on an approach established with the atelier 1 console (p. 32) from 1958, which had a combined radio and record player unit that was independent from the loudspeakers, the studio 2 comprised three separate components: the CS 11 combined preamplifier and record player, the CE 11 tuner and the CV 11 amplifier.

The system is characterized by well-proportioned metal boxes,

a reduction in forms to the rectangle and the circle, clear operation labelling and only three types of control switches, which are positioned according to their specific function. In 1961, the CS 11 record player was uncoupled from the preamplifier to form the PCS 4 (p. 76) and CSV 13 amplifier – allowing even more combinations to be created.

As Braun hi-fi systems developed, the modular principle continued to evolve, until receivers, preamplifiers, amplifiers, record players, tape recorders, video players, CD players and televisions were each turned into independent but technically and aesthetically compatible modules.

L 01, 1959
Auxiliary tweeter with stand
Dieter Rams
Braun

Loudspeaker: 18 × 18 × 8 cm (7 × 7 × 3 in);
stand: 123.5 × 26 cm (48½ × 10¼ in)
Loudspeaker: 1.3 kg (3 lb); stand:
5 kg (11 lb)

Laminated wood, steel
DM 45

The L 01 of 1959 was an auxiliary tweeter that could be combined with Ram's L 2 floor-standing speaker of the previous year (p. 37). With this design a new aesthetic was created using the elementary and asymmetric geometry of rectangle and line: a light grey box with black perforated grille is hung in parallel to the vertical stand. Its height can be adjusted for an optimum result depending on the listener's seating position, and the speaker box can also be removed entirely and placed on a shelf. The L 01's delicate composition is reminiscent of one of Alexander Calder's mobiles, but equally it shows inspiration from Eileen Gray's 1927 tube-light floor lamp. However, the suspended rectangle was a completely original design solution.

The loudspeaker's box-like enclosure soon became the template for Rams's bigger speaker designs, which began with the L 40 in 1961 (p. 78), and subsequently for all Braun loudspeaker models, as well as the majority of other manufacturers.

Also in the series: L 02 (1959), L 02 X (1960)

LE 1, 1959
Electrostatic loudspeaker with stand
Dieter Rams
Braun

76 × 83 × 31.5 cm (30 × 32½ × 12½ in)
21 kg (46¼ lb)

Metal, nickel-plated tubular steel
DM 795 each

The LE 1 loudspeaker of 1959 was
a redesign of the Quad ESL-57,
an electrostatic loudspeaker made
using innovative audio technology
developed by Peter Walker for the
British manufacturer Quad. Braun
licensed the technology and the basic
layout of the ESL-57; however, it was
only permitted to be sold in West
Germany. The British model consisted
of a fabric-covered frame, as was
usual for upholstered furniture at
the time, that stood on three tapered
wooden legs. In contrast, the LE 1
comprised a flat rectangular box set
in a grey metal frame, positioned on
an easel-like stand with a slight upward
inclination. The stand is made from
nickel-plated steel rods and the large

front surface of the speaker is covered
by a graphite-coloured, perforated
and curved metal grille. This curvature
is important from a design perspective
because it creates a gradation effect
in reflected light, giving the rectangular
shape a particular elegance. There is
also an intriguing contrast between
light and dark tones, and between bold
and delicate forms. The LE 1 was
revived by Quad Musikwiedergabe,
based near Koblenz, Germany, in 1999
and is currently being sold at a price
of almost €7,000 per pair. Only 500
pairs of speakers were manufactured
in the original run.

1960–1969

SK 6, 1960
Stereo radio-phono combination
Dieter Rams, Hans Gugelot
Braun

24 × 58.4 × 29.4 cm (9½ × 23 × 11½ in)
11.5 kg (25½ lb)

Metal, plastic, acrylic, rubber, elm
DM 448

The SK 6 brought stereophonic
sound to Braun audio products; its
integrated two-channel stereo amplifier
unit had 2 × 2 watts of power and
required an additional loudspeaker
to be connected. Rams reworked the
appearance of the record player,
replacing the organic lines of Gerd A
Müller's earlier tonearm design with
a more rectilinear form, and the rubber
nubs on the platter were replaced by
a continuous rubber strip. In technical
terms, the SK 6 represented a
meeting of the past and the future as
the speed controller could be set for
both shellac and modern stereophonic
records. The SK 61c export model had
a short-wave receiver instead of long-
wave and was distributed by Clairtone.

Also in the series: SK 61 (1961), SK 61c
(1962)

SM 3, 1960
Electric shaver
Gerd A Müller
Braun

10 × 7.3 × 3.4 cm (4 × 3 × 1½ in)
0.31 kg (¾ in)

Plastic, metal
DM 74

Building on the design of Rams and
Gerd A Müller's combi DL 5 shaver
from 1957 (p. 34), Müller further refined
the form and finish, narrowing the base
and opting for a completely smooth
surface. The power switch was also
moved to the opposite side, creating
a more balanced layout in relation to
the Braun logo. These changes would
set the standard for the sixtant SM 31
of 1962 (p. 102).

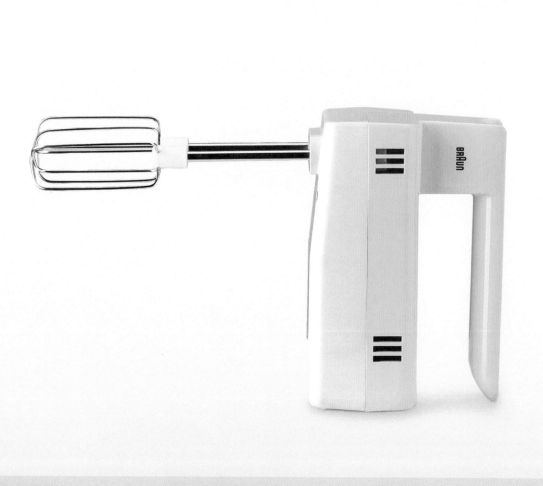

M 1 Multiquirl, 1960
Hand mixer
Gerd A Müller
Braun

15.6 × 10.8–27 × 7.3 cm
(6 × 4¼–10½ × 3 in)
0.8 kg (1¾ lb)

Plastic
DM 88 (price from 1962)

This hand mixer was one of the last designs produced by Gerd A Müller for Braun, and is a continuation of his work on the KM 3 (p. 35) and MX 3 (p. 45) kitchen appliances. In contrast to the subtly curving forms used in his previous designs, the M 1 hand mixer has a boxier appearance, which was possibly influenced by Rams. These same angular characteristics also distinguished it from its main competitor, the Krups 3 Mix, designed by Werner Glasenapp and released in 1959.

Also in the series: M 11 Multiquirl (1960)

F 22, 1960 / F 21, 1962 (pictured)
Electronic camera flash
Dieter Rams
Braun

6 × 8.5 × 7.5 cm (2½ × 3¼ × 3 in)
0.45 kg (1 lb)

Metal, plastic
DM 155

This compact, cube-shaped flash
unit demonstrates the continuing
miniaturization of such devices,
which, over the course of five years –
since Rams's EF 1 (p. 46) and
F 60 (p. 49) designs – had become
significantly smaller. This was
Braun's first camera-mounted flash
to contain the entire power unit.

Also in the series: F 20 (1961)

601 (RZ 60), 1960
Chair programme, low-back model
Dieter Rams
Vitsoe+Zapf / Vitsœ

70 × 60 × 65 cm (27½ × 23½ × 25½ in)
18 kg (39¾ lb)

Plastic, metal foil, foam, moulded latex,
die-cast aluminium, enamel; felt, nylon,
leather or fabric upholstery
DM 390 (price from 1973)

In 1960, two new modular furniture systems by Rams came onto the market, which differed significantly from the RZ 57 system he created in 1957 (pp. 27–9). While the previous designs were essentially box-like, for the RZ 60 programme Rams employed freer lines, which add a lightness to the form; the designer's use of more organic and curved silhouettes can be traced to this collection.

His chair designs are defined by two large cast-aluminium skid legs, which offer a high degree of stability, and the essentially rectangular seat and backrest construction has a pronounced backward tilt. The 601 is not intended for use at a table or desk, but for more relaxed seating. Rams's design notes state: 'Simple, inexpensive chair … unobtrusive so that several chairs can easily be grouped together, even in small apartments.' All the items in Rams's RZ 60 series are characterized by a visual lightness, which does not obstruct the room but instead enhances transparency.

602 (RZ 60), 1960
Chair programme, high-back model
Dieter Rams
Vitsoe+Zapf / Vitsœ

105 × 60 × 70 cm (41¼ × 23½ × 27½ in)
25 kg (55 lb)

Fibreglass-reinforced polyester resin,
die-cast aluminium, enamel; felt, nylon,
leather or fabric upholstery
DM 540 (price from 1973)

With the extension of the backrest
and the addition of a headrest, Rams's
601 chair (opposite) becomes a lounge
chair that is ideal for reading or
watching television. The tilting of the
seat front and headrest are as much
for comfort as they are to emphasize
the sculptural complexity of the chair
in the space.

601 / 602 (RZ 60), 1960
Side table
Dieter Rams
Vitsoe+Zapf / Vitsœ

37 × 60 × 53 cm (14½ × 23½ × 20¾ in)
12 kg (26½ lb)
Acrylic, fibreglass-reinforced polyester
resin or glass; die-cast aluminium; felt,

foam, leather or fabric upholstery
With acrylic table top: DM 168;
with glass table top: DM 298 (prices
from 1973)

To complement his 601 and 602
chairs, Rams used the same pair of
skid legs to design a matching side
table. It featured a large-format,
cast acrylic or glass table top, the
former of which had a rectangular
indentation in its surface. This unique
feature strengthens the table's
construction while also preventing
objects from rolling off. The side
table was complemented by an
upholstered stool, which can also
serve as a footrest for the chairs.

606 Universal Shelving System
(RZ 60), 1960
Shelving programme
Dieter Rams

Vitsoe+Zapf / sdr+ / De Padova / Vitsœ
Various sizes and weights

Anodized aluminium, powder-coated
sheet steel, lacquered wood or natural
wood veneer
Various prices

In 1960, Vitsoe+Zapf released a flexible and expandable shelving system.
It was initially named RZ 60, but since
1970 it has been known as the 606
Universal Shelving System, and it is still
in production today. The 606 is a truly
sophisticated example of design. The
basic structural element is a series of
E-track aluminium mounting rails,
which are perforated to allow the
attachment of shelves and units using
metal pins; the lateral rows of holes,
which often give other systems a more
industrial appearance, cannot be seen
from the front. Parallel-running grooves
allow fixtures to be inserted into
both sides of the rails in any position.
Base units and drawers were initially
veneered in light beech or American

walnut and fitted with aluminium side
panels. The drawers' front panels were
also available in a white laminate.

As with the RZ 57 system (p. 28), the
606 was designed to support Braun
hi-fi equipment perfectly; Vitsoe+Zapf
supplied holders that allowed audio
devices to be hung directly from the
E-profile tracks. Only four years after
its release, the 606 was put on display
at the *documenta III* international art
exhibition in Kassel.

The popularity of this system is
based on its restrained simplicity
and considerable flexibility that allows
every element to be adjusted to suit
the needs of the user. Over the years,

the original design has expanded
to include shelves, drawers, hanging
tables and cabinets catering to
practically every requirement. And
with every subsequent addition to the
series, care has been taken to ensure
that it is compatible with those that
came before it. With the exception
of the aluminium version – which
was licensed to Milan-based furniture
company De Padova from 1984 to
2016 – since 2012, the 606 has been
manufactured exclusively by Vitsœ in
Royal Leamington Spa, England, and
is successfully distributed worldwide.
Between 1995 and 2012, Rams's
design was also produced by the
Cologne-based company sdr+.

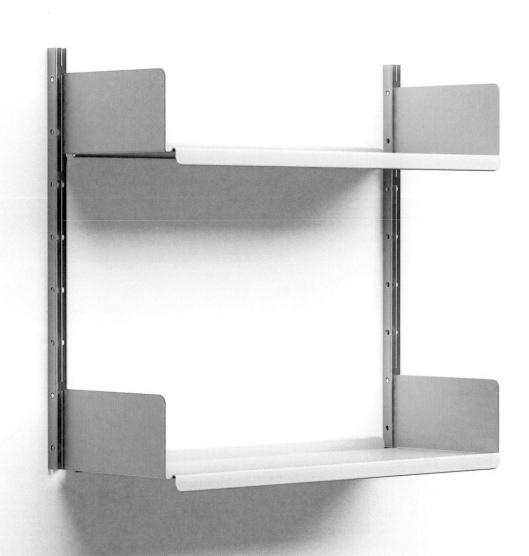

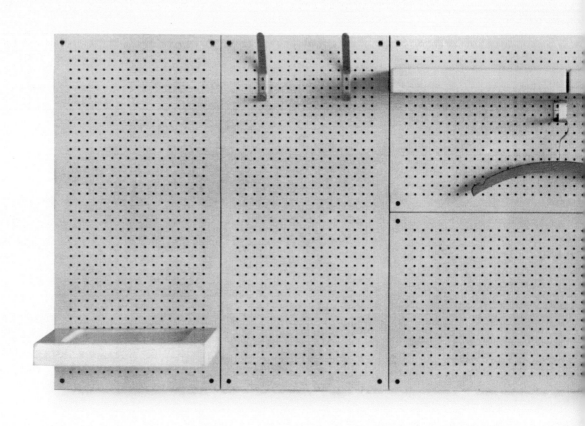

610, 1961
Wall panel system
Dieter Rams
Vitsoe+Zapf / Vitsœ / sdr+

80 × 40 × 2 cm
(31½ × 15¾ × ¾ in)
approx. 5 kg (11 lb)

Laminated sheet steel,
plastic, aluminium
DM 38–96

This extraordinary wall panel and
storage system consists of a series
of perforated steel sheets. The
80 x 40 cm (31 × 15½ in) panels can
be mounted to the wall horizontally
or vertically and combined as needed.
Different elements can be affixed
to the panels using screws, such as
coat hooks, glove storage, umbrella
stands and shelves.

D 40, 1961
Automatic slide projector
Dieter Rams
Braun

17.5 × 25.5 × 11 cm (7 × 10 × 4¼ in)
3.95 kg (8¾ lb)

Sheet steel, aluminium
DM 298

Following the limited release of the
D 50 projector in 1958 (p. 47), Rams
evolved the design further to create
an archetype that would continue to
be developed over the years. The D 40
was created with the assistance of
Braun designer Robert Oberheim, until
Oberheim took over the development
of the series in the 1970s. Its raised
rectangular box enclosure reflects the
design of the D 50, but here the hinged
tray guide is located on the right side,
parallel to the light and reflector. This
was the first Braun projector to use the
Leitz-designed slide trays that had
become industry standard.

Also in the series: D 45 (1965), D 47
(1966), D 46 and D 46 J (1967)

RT 20, 1961
Tabletop radio
Dieter Rams
Braun

25.6 × 50 × 18 cm (10 × 19¾ × 7 in)
7 kg (15½ lb)

Lacquered sheet steel, beech or pear wood veneer
DM 278

This tabletop radio is a continuation of the design used in the SK series. On the left are the slotted perforations of the radio's loudspeaker, two semi-circles that together form a whole. The thin, rectangular wooden box enclosure tapers slightly at the top so that the face tilts upwards towards the listener, giving elegance to the volume. This type of body construction resulted in a much better sound quality than that of the SK series. The lacquered metal fronts came in white or graphite shades. The RT 20 demonstrates how Braun products evolved to find a recognizable visual identity; it simultaneously references designs of the past, while the tapering anticipates the form of the audio devices that followed in the late 1970s. Approximately 6,600 units of the RT 20 radio were produced.

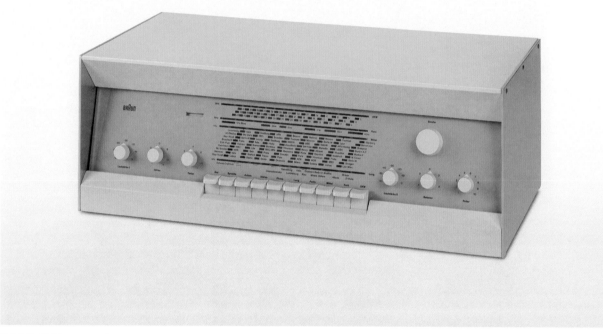

RCS 9, 1961
Stereo control unit
Dieter Rams
Braun

20.9 × 56.6 × 28 cm (8¼ × 22¼ × 11 in)
12 kg (26½ lb)

Lacquered wood, aluminium, glass,
plastic
DM 525

The enclosure for this combined
receiver and amplifier was largely
constructed of metal, the wooden
side panels used on the SK series
now replaced with aluminium sheets.
Designed without a record player,
the RCS 9 signalled an end to the
use of wood as a reference to
furniture. However, Rams retained
the sharp angles in the chassis that
were standard in earlier radio sets.
The stereo receiver was produced
in a run of 2,600 units.

CSV 13, 1961
Amplifier
Dieter Rams
Braun

11 × 40 × 32 cm (4¼ × 5¾ × 13 in)
11 kg (24¼ lb)

Sheet steel, aluminium, plastic
DM 775

The controls of this vacuum tube amplifier are arranged on a single level in an order that conveys their significance; the different input sources are activated using the pointed rotary switch on the left, and the sound quality is adjusted using the respective dials. The front side of the amplifier consists of an anodized aluminium plate fixed to the chassis with four visible screws. The body is made of sheet steel, lacquered in light grey or graphite. The lettering on the device is in lowercase, a nod to 1920s German Modernist design, and the warm incandescent light of the vacuum tubes could be seen through the ventilation slots on the top. The CSV 13, manufactured in a small run of 1,800 units, was later followed by the powerful CSV 60 model from 1962, a higher-end version better suited to more sophisticated hi-fi products. In a later development, the CSV 60-1 from 1967 featured a fourth toggle switch to put the tape recorder into read-after-write mode.

Also in the series: CSV 130 (1962), CSV 60 (1962), CSV 60-1 (1967)

PCS 4, 1961
Record player
Dieter Rams
Braun

13 × 30.8 × 21 cm (5 × 12 × 8¼ in)
2.5 kg (5½ lb)

Metal, plastic, rubber
DM 99

Continuing the lineage of the PC 3
record player (p. 30), this model
demonstrates a move towards the
more professional audio devices
of the time that supported larger
record player platters. A reworking
of the tonearm equipped the design
with a balance weight behind the
mounting mechanism, enabling the
stylus tracking force to be adjusted.

Also in the series: PCS 45 (1962),
PCS 46 (1963)

PCV 4, 1961
Portable stereo record player with
integrated amplifier
Dieter Rams

Braun
21 × 40 × 27 cm (8¼ × 15¾ × 10½ in)
3 kg (6½ lb)

Wood, fabric, metal, plastic, rubber
DM 368

This compact stereo record player
with two separate loudspeakers could
be packed into a portable case, making
it a more sophisticated successor
to the Phonokoffer PC 3 from 1956
(p. 31), in terms of both technology
and design. Similar to its predecessor,
the PCV 4's intended market was the
educational sector, as well as social
gatherings and parties.

L 40, 1961
Loudspeaker
Dieter Rams
Braun

56.6 × 24.3 × 28 cm (22¼ × 9½ × 11 in)
10 kg (22 lb)

Laminated wood, aluminium
DM 185

The L 40 heralded the introduction of a new loudspeaker archetype. Produced in a run of 4,000 units, the design comprises an elongated rectangular box with a white, graphite or walnut veneer finish that sits flush with a pressed aluminium mesh speaker grille. Positioned either vertically against a wall or horizontally on a shelf, the L 40 was unparalleled as far as consistency and minimalism were concerned. Braun's subsequent large-scale loudspeakers were subject to minor adjustments. The L 710 from 1969 had slightly rounded edges, while those on the atelier loudspeakers (p. 283) designed by Rams and Peter Hartwein in 1982 were chamfered at a 45-degree angle; but each design can be traced back to the basic form of the L 40. After designing the SK 4, with its distinctive upward-facing control panel and transparent acrylic cover, Rams succeeded for the second time in defining a universal typology for the audio industry.

Also in the series: L 40-1 (1964), L 20 (1962)

L 50, 1961
Bass reflex loudspeaker with stand
Dieter Rams
Braun

61 × 65 × 28 cm (24 × 25½ × 11 in)
14 kg (31 lb)

Laminated wood, aluminium, nickel-plated tubular steel
DM 295

For good sound you need a powerful loudspeaker; this large device delivered both bass and treble by means of different drivers while serving as a pedestal for an accompanying sound system.

Also in the series: L 60 and L 61 (1961), L 60-4 (1964)

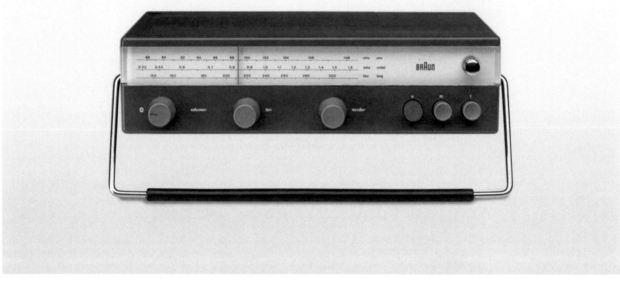

T 52, 1961
Portable radio
Dieter Rams
Braun

17 × 23 × 5.9 cm (6¾ × 9 × 2¼ in)
1.35 kg (3 lb)

Plastic, metal
DM 218

The T 52 was a reworking of Braun's
large and boxy transistor 1 radio
from 1957 (p. 36). In this version,
the rectangular enclosure was much
thinner and more compact, made
possible by the exclusive use of
transistors, and the tuning scale was
moved to the top to align with the
controls. Equipped with a swivelling
handle, the T 52 could be positioned
at an angle or mounted under the
dashboard of a car. The circular knobs
were lengthened, allowing them to be
operated without looking. The success
of the model inspired many variants.

Also in the series: T 54 (1961), T 520,
T 521, T 530 and T 540 (1962), T 510
and T 580 (1963)

atelier 3, 1962
Radio-phono combination
Dieter Rams
Braun

30.1 × 56.6 × 28 cm (12 × 22¼ × 11 in)
15 kg (33 lb)

Lacquered wood, aluminium, glass,
plastic, rubber
DM 685

The successor to the atelier 1 and 2
devices was given the same design
as the RCS 9 stereo control unit
(p. 74), although the tuning scale
was redesigned to remove the station
names. In addition, the PCS 4 record
player from 1961 (p. 76), which also
formed part of the SK 6 system (p. 58),
was integrated under a lacquered
wood cover.

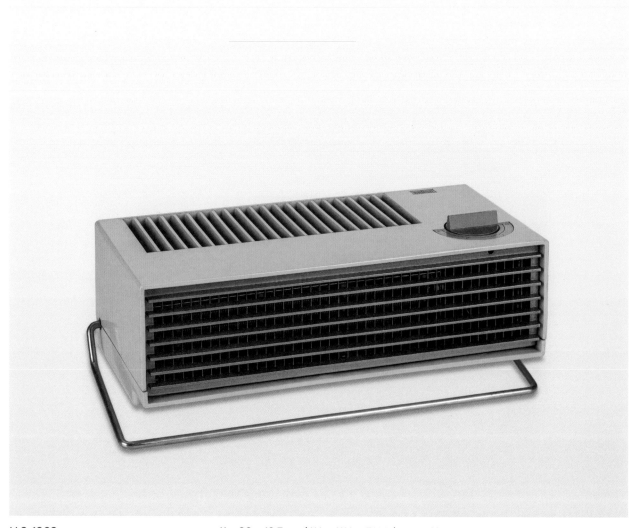

H 3, 1962
Fan heater with infrared remote control
Dieter Rams
Braun Española

11 × 29 × 13.5 cm (4¼ × 11½ × 5¼ in)
2.5 kg (5½ lb)

Sheet steel, steel, aluminium, plastic
DM 89

The H 3 fan heater was developed
by Braun Española and mainly
produced for the Spanish market.
Although a continuation of the 1959
model, the H 1 (p. 48), it is slimmer
and the switch is now prominently
positioned on the top. The blades of
the air outlet extend across the front
and are reflected by the air intake slots
positioned perpendicularly on top.
These graphic linear openings contrast
with the circular switch for a more
interesting aesthetic. The device can
be switched on and off with an infrared
remote control. The fan's rectangular
proportions resemble Braun's hi-fi
modules of the same period.

Also in the series: H 31 (1962)

D 20, 1962
Slide projector
Dieter Rams, Robert Oberheim
Braun

18 × 24.5 × 16.3 cm (7 × 9½ × 6½ in)
4.9 kg (10¾ lb)

Sheet steel, aluminium, plastic
DM 258

As a more affordable variant of the
D 40 projector (p. 72), this model has
no retractable slide-tray guide,
resulting in a wider construction and
a simpler technical approach. It was
produced at the request of Braun's
sales and marketing department as
a means to remain competitive in the
market. But even on a tighter budget,
there was no expense spared in terms
of design. Design at Braun always
involved a triangle of communication
between sales, the technicians and
the in-house design department.

Also in the series: D 21 (1964)

D 10, 1962
Slide projector
Dieter Rams, Robert Oberheim
Braun

This single-slide slide projector was
intended more for academic and
scientific purposes than for private
use. The front of the very narrow
cuboid is angled at the top, indicating
the orientation of the device.

15 × 24 × 8.5 cm (6 × 9½ × 3¼ in)
3 kg (6½ lb)

Sheet steel, plastic
DM 98

D 5 Combiscope, 1962
Slide projector/viewer
Dieter Rams
Braun

14.2 × 16.5 × 8 cm (5½ × 6½ × 3 in)
1.8 kg (4 lb)

Plastic, glass
DM 58.50

This compact device serves as both a slide projector and viewer. It also represents a completely new design approach, both conceptually and in terms of product semantics. The grey–green adjustable lens can be extended outwards from its light grey housing, thus indicating the different practical applications. The shift from horizontal projection to a 45-degree position is achieved by simply tilting the projector onto its slanted rear side.

Also in the series: D 6 (1963)

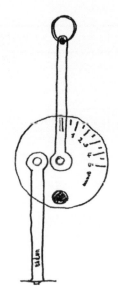

Tracking force gauge, 1962
Dieter Rams
Braun

7 cm (2¾ in) in diameter
0.02 kg (¾ oz)

Plastic, steel
DM 4.50

The stylus tracking force of hi-fi record players can be adjusted using a tonearm's built-in scale. But if you want to check whether the display on the tonearm is correct and to measure the exact weight in grams, you need the legendary Braun tracking force gauge. This sophisticated yet simple mechanical device consists of a white disc with a counterweight and red scale measuring from 0 to 8 grams (¼ oz); the Braun logo is unmissable against its bright yellow background. Though small, this gauge was a true reflection of Rams's holistic approach to design: as simple as possible, using as little design as possible, and with as much precision as possible.

T 41, 1962
Pocket radio
Dieter Rams
Braun

8.2 × 14.8 × 4 cm (3¼ × 5¾ × 2 in)
0.45 kg (1 lb)

Plastic, acrylic
DM 135

This third pocket radio was given the same concentric loudspeaker grille as its predecessor, the T 4 (p. 50), but the tuning window was enlarged into a partial circle to reveal the frequencies for the three airwave bands and an ultra-thin pointer, creating the impression of a highly precise technical device. Aside from the off-white body, the Minimalist colour scheme includes a blue switch and red tuning wheel. In homage to this now-iconic series of products, Northern Irish rock band Rams' Pocket Radio, a project led by musician Peter J McCauley, released the 2011 song 'Dieter Rams Has Got the Pocket Radios'.

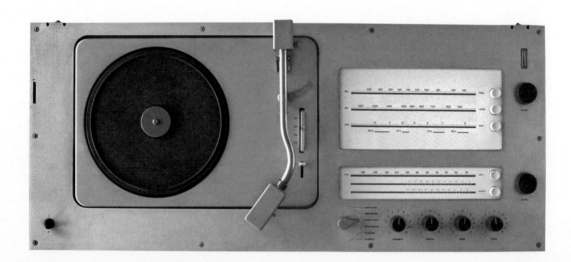

audio 1, 1962
Radio-phono combination
Dieter Rams
Braun

16 × 64.7 × 28 cm (6¼ × 25½ × 11 in)
16.5 kg (36½ lb)

Sheet steel, aluminium, plastic, acrylic
DM 1,090

With this compact, integrated device, comprising a radio, amplifier and record player, Rams brought cutting-edge technology into the 1960s home. However, the audio 1 sound system was anything but hi-tech. Embracing the aesthetics of the time, elements were designed to reflect their function. Push-button controls were made concave in order to stop fingers from slipping when they were pressed. All level settings are controlled by circular knobs: large for the wave-band and small for volume, tone and balance. The rotary switch, with its somewhat organic, teardrop shape, is given a prominent, central position. In this element we also see a contrast with the design's overall rectangular

form, similar to the way in which the red, yellow or green dot of the master switch used on many Braun devices contrasts with their otherwise monochromatic appearance.

The overall layout of the stereo is clear and concise, and is more comparable to the Swiss typography of the time than with other German radios. Although the combination of aluminium casing, plastic buttons and a transparent acrylic cover – as well as deliberately visible screws – might usually be considered unsophisticated, Rams succeeded in using them to create an extremely valuable, and at the same time contemporary, product. Unlike Hans Gugelot and Herbert

Lindinger's futuristic spaceship, the studio 1, designed for Braun in 1957, Rams's audio 1 can be seen as the expression of a new era and a successful attempt to make optimum use of humble materials. Compared to its predecessor from the HfG Ulm, every part looks light and bright. The aluminium plate was lacquered to give it a silky matt finish; the plastic parts were precision-made; the tonearm, with its round balance weight, gives the impression of top performance; and the reflective acrylic cover adds a distinct lightness.

Also in the series: audio 1 M (1962)

PCS 51, 1962 / PCS 5, 1962 (pictured)
Record player
Dieter Rams
Braun

20 × 40 × 32 (8 × 15¾ × 12½ in)
10 kg (22 lb)

Sheet steel, wood, aluminium, plastic,
rubber, acrylic
DM 546 (PC 5)

This sophisticated record player was
the first Braun device to be specifically
developed to meet hi-fi standards, at
a time when other audio components
were simply being upgraded. With this
design Rams created the basic shape
that was to define all subsequent
Braun hi-fi devices: a smooth-sided
box with controls on the top, a large
platter and a transparent acrylic dust
cover. The acrylic cover of these early
devices could only be bent in two
directions, so the sides were initially
left open. Later, dust covers were
produced using thermo injection
moulding and could be closed on all
sides. The PCS 52 model came with
a high-performance 3009 tonearm
manufactured by the British company

SME, which incorporated an
anti-skating guide and additional
balance weight.

Also in the series: PCS 52, PCS 5 A
and PC 5 (1962) PCS 5-37 (1963),
PCS 52-E (1965)

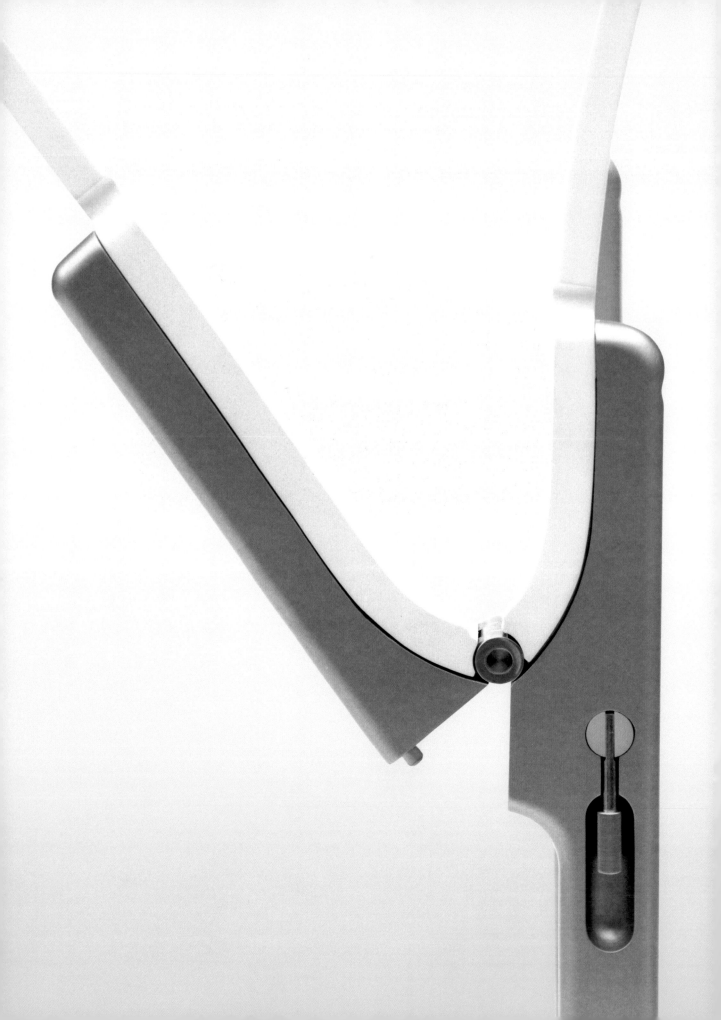

Prototype for a folding chair, 1962
Dieter Rams
Vitsoe+Zapf

Size and weight unknown

Die-cast aluminium, plastic
Not released for sale

In 1962, Rams developed a two-legged, skid-base chair for Vitsoe+Zapf that featured a folding seat and could be connected with others to form row seating. The chairs were stackable for easy storage and the furniture company planned to create a wall-mounting attachment as well. The construction is similar to that used on Rams's cantilever stand system (p. 145) developed in 1967 for Braun. However, Vitsoe+Zapf was unable to resolve issues of damage that resulted from folding the chair, so the design was never realized.

622, 1962
Chair programme, low-back model
Dieter Rams
Vitsoe+Zapf / Vitsœ

78 × 55 × 55 cm (30¾ × 21¾ × 21¾ in)
12 kg (26½ lb)

Fibreglass, foam, leather or fabric,
die-cast aluminium
DM 286–698 (prices from 1980)

A chair with a well-designed seat
shell should deliver an ergonomically
convincing result. In this respect,
Rams's 622 chair is successful and
particularly suited to sitting at a table.
Its relatively heavy frame was due to
cost; to use a lighter metal alloy would
have been twice as expensive.

620 (RZ 62), 1962
Chair programme, high-back model
with footstool
Dieter Rams

Vitsoe+Zapf / sdr+ / Vitsœ
92 × 66 × 79 cm (36¼ × 26 × 31 in)
approx. 50 kg (110 lb)

Beech, metal, sheet moulding
compound, leather or fabric
DM 1,960–2,080 (prices from 1973)

In addition to the 606 Universal
Shelving System (pp. 65–9), in 1961
Rams began work on a seating system
for Vitsoe+Zapf. Taking inspiration from
the rectangular geometry of furniture
created by Gerrit Rietveld and Mart
Stam in the early twentieth century,
as well as the more organic forms used
by mid-century American designers
Charles and Ray Eames, Rams developed his 620 chair programme as
a series of soft cubes. The basic
construction of this extraordinarily
comfortable armchair comprises
a wooden frame and coil-sprung core,
set into fibreglass-reinforced plastic
shells. The seat and back cushions
are stuffed with down feathers and
upholstered in fabric or leather.

Front ball castors and rear feet make
the armchair easy to reposition;
alternatively, it can be mounted on a
swivel – a ball-bearing turntable made
of anodized aluminium with a base
plate – and rotated in all directions.
The individual armchairs can be
converted into sofas of any width by
dismantling the arms and joining them
together using a connecting plate
bracket, resulting in a fully modular
system. The 620 is a piece of furniture
that takes into consideration functional
geometric room design as well as a
user's physical requirements. In 1973,
a legal dispute led to the German
Federal Court of Justice granting the
chair system copyright protection,
considering it to be a work of art.

94

620 (RZ 62), 1962
Chair programme, low-back model
Dieter Rams
Vitsoe+Zapf / sdr+ / Vitsœ

77 × 66 × 79 cm (30¼ × 26 × 31 in)
approx. 45 kg (99¼ lb)

Beech, metal, sheet moulding
compound, leather or fabric
DM 1,770–1,870 (prices from 1973)

As well as the 620 series high-back armchair, Rams designed a low-back version, and made the two pieces interchangeable. For this purpose, two special flat screws, visible on either side of the chair, must be loosened. These 'pig-nose' screws are the same type as those used in the T 3 pocket radio from 1956 (pp. 42–3), offering another example of Rams's ability to seamlessly transfer design details from one product to another. Not only do the screws serve a technical purpose, they also add a functional aesthetic. Both chair configurations are today back in production by Vitsœ.

620, c.1962
Table
Dieter Rams
Vitsoe+Zapf / Vitsœ

37.5 × 65.5 × 65.5 cm
(14¾ × 25¾ × 25¾ in)
8 kg (17½ lb)

Plastic
DM 1,145–1,190

This flat coffee table was created to
accompany the 620 chair programme
(pp. 94–5). The furniture comprises
several plastic parts and features
the same surface indentation as the
621 stool/side table (opposite). For
assembly, the legs were inserted into
sockets in the table top. The design
was given the same width and depth
as the 620 models so that it could be
inserted between two armchairs or
used as a corner unit.

621, 1962
Side table/nesting tables/stool
Dieter Rams
Vitsoe+Zapf / Vitsœ

Large: 45 × 52.5 × 32 cm (17¾ × 20½
× 12½ in); small: 36 × 46.5 × 30 cm
(14 × 18¼ × 11¾ in)
Large: 5.5 kg (12 lb); small: 4.5 kg (10 lb)

Plastic
Large: DM 190; small: DM 175

The 621 side table was a natural addition to Rams's 620 chair programme (pp. 94–5). The U-shaped pieces were given a flat upper surface and indentations on the sides, reflecting those used on the 601/602 table and footstool from 1960 (p. 64). Internal bracing was added, allowing the three sides to be thinner and resulting in a wider internal radius. The table was manufactured using injection moulding to produce a lightweight and stable construction; adjustable screw feet allowed for further stability on uneven floors. The table was originally manufactured by Vitsoe+Zapf from 1962 to 1995, then revived again in by Vitsœ in 2014; it was also available as a nesting pair. With this table-cum-stool, Rams continued the tradition set by Marcel Breuer's tubular steel nesting tables (1925–6) and the Ulm Stool (1954–5) by Max Bill and Paul Hildinger of the HfG Ulm, but created a distinct and convincing solution in plastic. The larger table can turned on its side and used as a tray table for the sofa or a bed.

Wall-mounted sound system, 1962
Dieter Rams
Braun

28 × 136.2 × 10.5 cm (11 x 53½ × 4 in)
Various weights

Sheet steel, aluminium, plastic
See individual models for further
specifications

Mounting a sound system on a wall
like a piece of art was unusual in
mid-1960s Germany, but this approach
would later be capitalized on by brands
such as Bang & Olufsen. The Braun
hi-fi separates that make up this
system – the L 45 loudspeakers (p. 100),
TS 40 amplifier/tuner (p. 101) and TG
60 tape recorder (pp. 132–3) – could
be placed individually on a table or
shelf, but only when displayed together
on a wall do they reveal their particular
appeal. This modular approach to
audio design was initiated in a study
by Herbert Lindinger and Hans
Gugelot at the HfG Ulm for Braun in
1959 with the title 'A Modular Design
for Acoustic and Visual Information
Storage and Transfer Devices in
Living Quarters'. However, the study
only focused on the idea of an entire
system and not the specific design
of the individual components. Rams
began the development of such a
system in 1960, designing each of the
elements in turn.

L 45, 1962 / L 450, 1965 (pictured)
Loudspeakers
Dieter Rams
Braun

28 × 47.2 × 10.5 cm (11 × 18½ × 4 in)
6 kg (13¼ lb)

Laminated wood, anodized aluminium
DM 267

These loudspeakers were adapted
to accompany the flat design of the
TS 40 amplifier/tuner (opposite),
allowing a pair of them to be mounted
with the integrated device on a wall
as a triptych. The L 450 model from
1965 was produced in an impressive
run of 22,000 units.

Also in the series: L 25 and L 46 (1963),
L 450-1 (1967), L 450-2 (1968), L 470
(1969), L 310 (1970)

TS 40, 1962 / TS 45, 1964 (pictured)
Amplifier/tuner
Dieter Rams
Braun

28 × 47 × 10.5 cm (11 × 18½ × 4 in)
11 kg (24¼ lb)

Sheet steel, aluminium, plastic
DM 1,145

In terms of both technical performance and design, the TS 40 and
TS 45 combined amplifiers/tuners
represented an uncoupling from
the audio 1 sound system (p. 88).
The ventilation slots on the left
balanced the device's proportions
and, ultimately, made it distinct from
its previous form, while the light
green power button featured on all of
Braun's later audio devices. Produced
in a run of 4,200 units, the control
unit could be positioned on a shelf
or other surface, and the TS 45 model
could be mounted on a wall as part
of Rams's wall-mounted sound
system (pp. 98–9).

sixtant SM 31, 1962
Electric shaver
Gerd A Müller, Hans Gugelot
Braun

10 × 7.3 × 3.4 cm (4 × 3 × 1¼ in)
0.31 kg (¾ lb)

Plastic, metal
DM 94

After Gerd A Müller left Braun in 1960,
the company's engineers developed
an extremely thin shaving foil that was
perforated with miniature hexagonal
openings – and they needed a shaver
design to pair it with. Starting from
Müller's SM 3 (p. 59), Hans Gugelot
switched the traditional white casing
for a brushed black version and chose
a matt chrome-plated finish for the
shaving head. This was a departure
from the clinical white shades associated with bathroom design in the
1950s and early 1960s, towards
a product that was not only functional
but also had strong aesthetic appeal.
Approximately eight million units of the
SM 31 were produced.

FS 1000, 1962
Prototype for a portable television set
Dieter Rams
Braun

37.5 × 30 × 25.5 cm (14¾ × 11¾ × 10 in)
6 kg (13¼ lb)

Aluminium, plastic, glass
Not released for sale

At the same time as Rams was developing his T 1000 world-band receiver (p. 106), which came onto the market in 1963, he was also working on a portable television set. As with his first prototypes for the receiver (pp. 104–5), Rams chose a vertical rectangular box as the basic shape. The loudspeaker was positioned over the monitor and the controls were placed underneath. Four rotary switches and two slide switches kept operation simple. At the time, there were only two television channels in West Germany: ARD and ZDF; a third was added in 1964.

The TV's cathode-ray tube bulges slightly at the front to create a rounded screen, a feature that became the standard for Braun floor-standing television sets. The screen is no longer masked by safety glass, as was used on many competing products, but is shown in its entirety, including the black border. This aesthetic shared parallels with a style of photography where the entire negative is visible, sometimes including the sprocket holes, indicating that the photograph has not been manipulated. In a similar way, the frame around the television screen communicates that this is not a literal window into the world but information transmitted by technology.

In another nod to the T 1000 radio, the TV's loudspeaker grille is made of

finely perforated sheeting, and an aluminium cover is attached to the device to protect it during transport. The cover also contains a compartment for storing the operating instructions. Unfortunately, the FS 1000 proved too ahead of its time in terms of the available technology; the deep picture tube resulted in an unfortunate hump at the back of the portable device, which discouraged the company from pursuing the project. Braun management was slow in spotting a market for portable television sets, but the competition would quickly seize the opportunity.

Prototypes for the T 1000 world-band
receiver, 1962
Dieter Rams
Braun

Specifications unknown
Not released for sale

In the early 1960s, Erwin Braun
developed the idea of 'Grand Design',
a term he used to describe high-end
design and technology in electronic
devices; the T 1000 was a direct
result of this initiative. World-band
radio receivers already existed in the
United States, such as Zenith Radio's
Trans-Oceanic from 1957, but they
were mostly used by the army during
international missions to receive
broadcasts from home. Short-wave
radio receivers were also popular
with radio enthusiasts at the time as
a means of receiving news from across
the world.

No expense was spared in the
development of the Braun world-band

receiver; Rams was given free rein
by company management in terms
of both technical and design development, and the use of materials.
At the same time as designing the
T 1000, he also created a portable
television set, the FS 1000 (p. 103).
On both devices, the speaker needed
to be placed at the top to allow the
device to stand upright. Sketches and
photos of the T 1000 and FS 1000
prototypes have been preserved in
the Rams Archive, and one of these
prototypes of the TV set forms part
of the collection of the Museum
Angewandte Kunst (Museum of
Applied Arts) in Frankfurt am Main.
However, the original prototypes of
the radio have not survived.

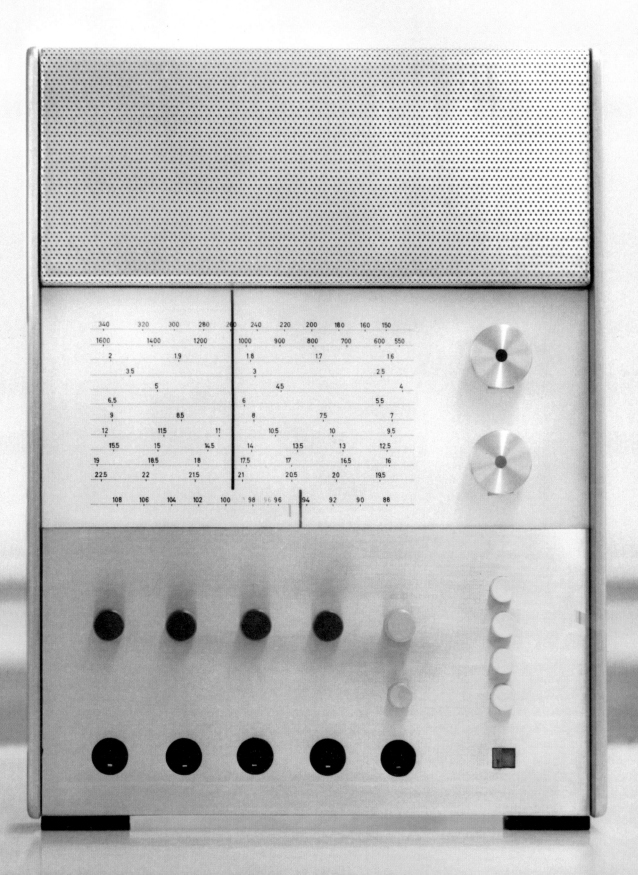

T 1000, 1963
World-band receiver
Dieter Rams
Braun

25 × 36 × 13.5 cm (25¾ × 14¼ × 5¼ in)
7 kg (15½ lb)

Wood, anodized aluminium, artificial
leather, plastic
DM 1,400

By the early 1960s, West Germany
was gradually emerging from the
isolation caused by the Nazi regime
and World War II. In what seemed to
be a reflection of cosmopolitanism and
mobility, the T 1000 radio's design was
suited to the times, and it later became
emblematic of Rams's own approach.
From a simple wooden box veneered
in aluminium, a hinged panel opens to
reveal an elaborate interface complete
with striking black tuning scale, and
a series of knobs, switches and
connection sockets – a complex scene
that stands in stark contrast to the
plain exterior.

True to form, every aspect of Rams's
design addresses function:

FM operation is indicated through
the uniform red of the power button,
tuning knob and scale lettering; all
the controls are clearly and logically
arranged, and sized to suit the hand;
the rotary bandswitch on the side feels
substantial; and the comprehensive
operating manual has its own compartment in the front hinged panel. The
large, detailed scale alludes to the
precision of the instrument itself, and,
with its ultra-fine typography and
clear numbering, is a prime example
of meticulous design. Despite all the
technical and functional complexity,
Rams succeeded in achieving a high
degree of elegance and aesthetic
quality. When the front panel is closed,
the T 1000 hints at the contemporary

design aesthetics of the Apple
products that arrived forty years later.

Created in collaboration with chief
engineer Joachim Fahrendholz and
design engineer Harald Haupenberger,
the device represents the peak of
German engineering achievement. Due
to increased demand from numerous
German embassies that were keen to
use the radio as an exemplar of national
design and technical ingenuity, after
an initial run of 11,300 units the device
was updated with a leather handle and
re-released as the T 1000 CD in 1968.

Also in the series: TN 1000 power
supply unit (1963), T 1000 CD (1968)

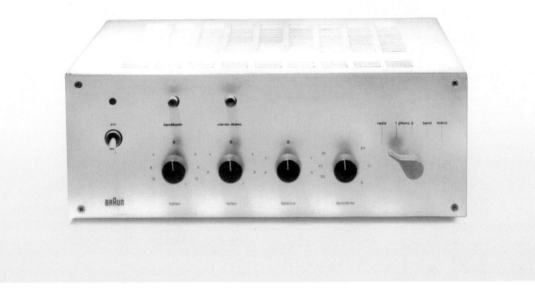

CSV 10, 1962 / CSV 12, 1966 (pictured)
Amplifier
Dieter Rams
Braun

10 × 28.5 × 28.2 cm (4 × 11¼ × 11 in)
5.8 kg (12¾ lb)

Sheet steel, aluminium, plastic
DM 558

Braun's first amplifier module built using transistor technology drew inspiration from the audio 1 compact sound system (p. 88), but its design and construction were based on the previous year's CSV 13 tube amplifier (p. 75). While its performance was not quite comparable to that of the CSV 60 tube amplifier, also released in 1962, it does feature the elegant, teardrop-shaped rotary switch that debuted with the audio 1, and toggle switches have been removed.

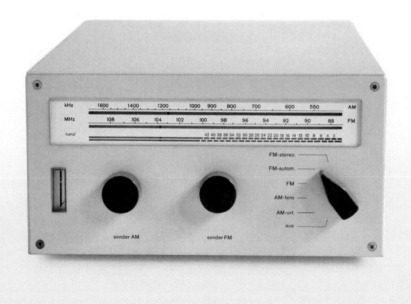

CET 15, 1963
Medium-wave and FM tuner
Dieter Rams
Braun

11 × 20 × 33 cm (4¼ × 8 × 13 in)
4.5 kg (10 lb)

Sheet steel, aluminium, acrylic
DM 568

Similar to the CSV 10 amplifier (p. 107), the tuner from Rams's modular hi-fi series has an industrial look: the visible screws on the front panel are a key part of the aesthetic, and the triangular setting switch reflects the form found on the older CSV 13 model (p. 75). Such features are reminiscent of technical measuring instruments. This model was the first Braun device to boast an automatic FM tuner.

Also in the series: CE 16 (1964)

SK 55, 1963
Mono radio-phono combination
Dieter Rams, Hans Gugelot
Braun

24 × 58.4 × 29.4 cm (9½ × 23 × 11½ in)
11.5 kg (25½ lb)

Metal, plastic, acrylic, ash
DM 438

The last of Braun's 'Snow White's Coffin' series was a mono device and had 3 watts of power. As with the previous SK designs, the 55 was reworked by Rams; the record player was given a new lightweight tonearm made of bent aluminium and a large graphite-coloured rubber platter, with matching switches and knobs. Rams also altered the design of the speed selector switch. Only the tuner knob was left white, with the addition of a red dot that emphasized its function in relation to the tuning scale. Across the full SK range, an estimated 70,000 units were produced.

PS 2, 1963
Record player
Dieter Rams
Braun

10 × 31 × 22.5 cm (4 × 12¼ × 8¾ in)
2.5 kg (5½ lb)

Sheet steel, aluminium, plastic, rubber
DM 98

Braun's last small-scale record player, the PS 2, came integrated into the SK 55 (p. 109) and TC 20 sound systems (p. 112), but it was also offered as a standalone unit. Unlike some of the company's larger devices, it had a more lightweight structure, but it still retained the familiar box-like shape. Produced in a small run of 2,900 units, the PS 2 is undoubtedly Braun's sleekest and most elegant model from its early series of record players.

TC 20, 1963
Stereo radio-record player combination
Dieter Rams
Braun

14.5 × 52 × 24 cm (5¾ × 20½ × 9½ in)
9 kg (19¾ lb)

Sheet steel, aluminium, plastic, rubber,
acrylic
DM 795

In 1963, Braun developed a smaller
and less powerful radio-and-record-
player combination as an inexpensive
alternative to the audio 1 system of the
previous year (p. 88). Featuring the PS 2
record player (pp. 110–11), which was
also sold as a separate unit, the TC 20
system required an additional decoder
to be installed for stereophonic reception. Instead of the aluminium used on
the audio 1, the upper surface of the
device is covered in sheet steel; the
teardrop-shaped rotary switch has also
been replaced, as this particular
design element was initially used to
distinguish top-of-the-range devices.

F 25 hobby, 1963
Electronic camera flash
Dieter Rams
Braun

4 × 10.5 × 8 cm (1½ × 4 × 3 in)
0.25 kg (½ lb)

Plastic, metal
DM 195 (F 26 hobby)

Since the debut of Braun's first flash unit, the Hobby de Luxe, in 1953, the photography market had become a thriving mainstay for the company. However, this initial design still resembled the early flash holders that carried magnesium bulbs. With the advent of the electronic flash, along with the increasing miniaturization of electronics in the early 1960s, a new compact, one-piece form became possible. Rams began with a cube-shaped housing that could be shoe-mounted directly on to the camera (p. 61), but this soon evolved into the elongated box design that would become Braun's standard for some time after.

Also in the series: F 26 hobby (1963)

FA 3, 1963
Double-8 movie camera
Dieter Rams, Richard Fischer, Robert Oberheim

Braun Nizo
14.9 × 21.5 × 6.5 cm (6 × 8½ × 2½ in)
1.5 kg (3¼ lb)

Metal, plastic, imitation leather
DM 798–1,098

In 1962, Braun acquired the renowned Munich-based camera manufacturer Niezoldi & Krämer. This was accompanied by a radical redesign of the company's products, carried out at Braun's Frankfurt factory. Before this, Nizo cameras still featured the industrial aesthetics of the 1930s, with many confusing adjustment knobs. The designers in Frankfurt simplified the user interface and opted for a facade of silver-lacquered metal combined with black imitation leather or plastic. The FA 3 is another early example of this silver-and-black combination, which had already been used for the HT 1 toaster of 1961, by Braun designer Reinhold Weiss, and the sixtant SM 31 shaver of 1962

(p. 102), and became an essential design feature of many Braun devices. Like its predecessors (pictured above left), the camera was designed for double-8 mm film – a 16 mm film exposed in two halves and then divided by a photo laboratory. It had a spring-wound drive mechanism, which was operated using a large, partially retractable hand crank. The FA 3 came with modern Variogon zoom lenses manufactured by Jos. Schneider Optische Werke (now Schneider Kreuznach) in Bad Kreuznach, Germany.

EA 1 electric, 1964
Electric double-8 movie camera
Dieter Rams, Richard Fischer
Braun Nizo

9.5 × 23.7 × 6 cm (3¾ × 9¼ × 2½ in)
1.3 kg (3 lb)

Aluminium, plastic, imitation leather
DM 698

This sleek movie camera, newly fitted with an electric motor, would go on to define the basic shape and structure of nearly all future Braun Nizo designs: a long, thin rectangular box with an integrated, folding handle. It came in a heavy die-cast aluminium housing with black imitation leather on both sides, and the semi-circular frame counter display was adopted from the preceding model (opposite). The EA 1 was designed for everyone, and required no technical understanding; the automatic exposure meant that only small adjustments were necessary. Later models featuring the new Super-8 film magazine were upgraded with lighter aluminium side panels and were largely designed by Robert Oberheim. Combined with the basic shape and structure established by the EA 1 camera, Oberheim's Nizo S 8 from 1965 (p. 135) became the template for the final form and material aesthetics of all subsequent Braun movie cameras, with the exception of a few entirely black models. In April 1970, Nizo was officially incorporated into the Braun brand, but it was subsequently sold again at the end of 1981 to Bosch, which soon dissolved the company.

HTK 5, 1964
Freezer
Dieter Rams
Braun

47.5 × 53 × 60 cm (18¾ × 21 × 23½ in)
18 kg (39¾ lb)

Sheet steel, aluminium, plastic
Price unknown

This small freezer was the result of
an idea from Braun's sales department
to open up a new product segment.
Rams only played a small part in its
design, mainly concerning the handle
and ventilation slots. The company
would soon discontinue the range.

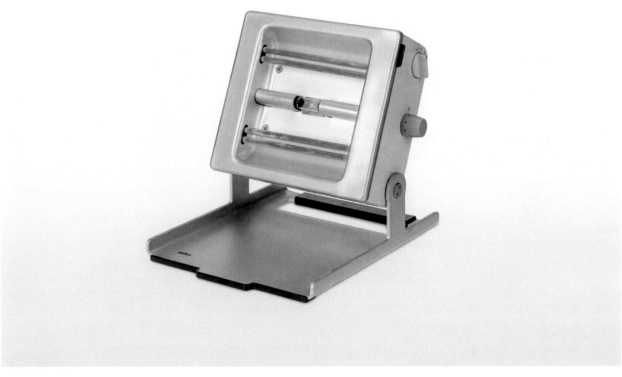

HUV 1, 1964
Infrared lamp
Dieter Rams, Reinhold Weiss,
Dietrich Lubs

Braun
6.7 × 16.8 × 20.5 cm (2½ × 6½ × 8 in)
0.95 kg (2 lb)

Aluminium, plastic
DM 129

This innovative sunlamp was designed
for easy transport; when folded, the
stand also functions as a cover with
an integrated handle. Rams opted for
the same pig-nose screws as those
used in the T 3 pocket radio from
1958 (pp. 42–3) and the 620 chair
programme from 1962 (pp. 94–5).
The rotary knobs also reference the
ones used on earlier Braun products.

EF 300, 1964
Electronic camera flash
Dieter Rams
Braun

Power unit: 14.2 × 19.3 × 5.9 cm
(5½ × 7½ × 2¼ in); flash unit:
22 × 9.8 × 9.8 cm (8¾ × 4 × 4 in)
2.5 kg (5½ lb)

Plastic, glass
DM 368–498

This flash unit was intended for semi-professional use. In order to produce a high-strength output, a large external power unit was required, which had practically the same volume and shape as the EF 1 from 1958 (p. 46). The flash head with handle is connected to the power unit via a coiled cable, allowing it to be detached for increased flexibility, which was particularly useful for photojournalism.

FP 1, 1964
Slim film projector
Dieter Rams, Robert Oberheim
Braun Nizo

16.9 × 29 × 12 cm (6¾ × 11½ × 4¾ in)
4 kg (8¾ lb)

Metal, plastic
DM 546

In addition to its movie cameras, Braun produced and sold film projectors. Its first device, the FP 1, was designed jointly by Rams and Robert Oberheim, although all subsequent models were developed primarily by Oberheim. Rams would often collaborate with a colleague from the design team to develop new product types, before handing over the project for them to manage. The FP 1 features Braun's distinctive slotted air outlet grille, a prominent black rotary control switch and the same black accent for the lens. The functions on the operator's side are clearly divided into several vertical panels; the design does not feature the fully enclosed casing that would soon become standard for Braun projectors.

Also in the series: FP 1 S (1965)

FS 80, 1964
Black-and-white television set
Dieter Rams
Braun

66.5 × 59 × 37.5 cm (26¼ × 23¼ × 14¾ in)
35 kg (77¼ lb)

Laminated wood, plastic, aluminium
DM 1,590

Whether placed on a table or used as a free-standing device on a stand, this television set, with its curved, fully visible picture screen, clearly draws on the design of its predecessor, the FS 1000 prototype from 1962 (p. 103). The loudspeaker and the controls are located in a lower panel below the screen, where the slotted speaker grille is also placed. Following Hans Gugelot's first TV design for Braun in 1955, which featured a visible wooden chassis, the FS 80 presents an elegant and clearly defined form that could be equated with the 'bel design' culture being championed by the Italian design industry and companies such as Olivetti during the 1960s. The FS 80 was produced in a run of 3,000 units.

Also in the series: FS 80-1 (1965–6)

audio 2, 1964
Hi-fi radio-phono combination
Dieter Rams
Braun

16 × 64.7 × 28 cm (6¼ × 25½ × 11 in)
18 kg (39¾ lb)

Sheet steel, aluminium, plastic, acrylic
DM 1,590

Braun's audio 2 sound system came with a fully redesigned record player featuring a large platter. The PS 400, which was also offered as a stand-alone unit from 1965 (p. 128), came fully integrated into the aluminium framework, a feature that became the standard in Braun's later audio devices. This was a considerable advance over its predecessor, the audio 1 (p. 88), whose record player still resembled that of the SK 4 series. During production, the device's wiring was stowed in a trough in the base so that it was not visible at the rear of the free-standing unit.

Each successive model in the 'audio' series – ranging from audio 2/3 to

audio 310 – only had minor adjustments made to it, but each was improved in terms of performance. Manufactured in runs of up to 16,400 units (audio 310), the compact sound systems were produced until 1973. In 1970, *Phono Form* magazine described the series as, 'Audio by Braun: the VW Beetle of the German hi-fi industry'; however, this sound system was a third of the price of a VW Beetle.

Also in the series: audio 2/3 (1965), audio 250 (1967), audio 300 (1969), audio 310 (1971)

HZ 1, 1965
Room thermostat
Dieter Rams
Braun

10.5 × 6 × 3 cm (4 × 2½ × 1 in)
0.2 kg (½ lb)

Plastic, acrylic
DM 34

Rams designed this small room
thermostat for use with fan heaters.
Featuring vertical slots at both
ends, and a rotary switch with semi-
circular scale, the device allowed
users to switch off energy-intensive
appliances automatically once there
was enough heat.

H 6, 1965
Convection heater
Dieter Rams, Richard Fischer
Braun

40 × 64 × 16 cm (15¾ × 25 × 6¼ in)
7 kg (15½ lb)

Steel, aluminium, plastic
DM 194

This large, free-standing rectangular unit contains two heating systems. First, it can be used as a convection heater, releasing the generated heat through the slotted air outlet at the top, similar to a radiator, and allowing heat to circulate throughout the room. Alternatively, a fan heater with tangential blower can blow hot air forwards, offering a more direct heat source. The heater is raised on a cantilever stand, removing the need for front legs, and allowing the air inlet to be positioned underneath. This construction also makes it appear to float slightly above the floor.

KM 2 Multiwerk, with KMZ 2 citrus
juicer and KMK 2 coffee grinder
attachments, 1965
Kitchen appliance system

Dieter Rams, Richard Fischer
Braun
Without attachments:
16.2 × 19.2 × 9.7 cm (6½ × 7½ × 3¾ in)

1.3 kg (3 lb)
Plastic, metal
DM 198

The KM 2 Multiwerk was developed
in response to a suggestion from Artur
Braun, who wanted an alternative to
Braun's larger kitchen appliance
system, the KM 3 from 1957 (p. 35).
Intended as a highly functional, entry-
level appliance for a small household,
the combination hand mixer and
blender comprised a motor and
gearbox housed in a cylindrical unit,
onto which the blender and mixer
attachments could be fixed.

Bottle for shaver cleaning fluid, 1965
Dieter Rams
Braun

13.8 × 5.5 cm in diameter (5½ × 2 in)
0.15 kg (¼ lb)

Glass, plastic
DM 4

Designing a bottle for shaver
cleaning fluid may sound trivial, but
in this solution by Rams, the seamless
transition between cap and glass,
in combination with the left-aligned
text, give the bottle a no-nonsense
appeal that perfectly matches Braun's
shaver range.

F 200, 1965 / F 100, 1966 (pictured)
Electronic camera flash
Dieter Rams
Braun

9.5 × 3.3 × 7 cm (3¾ × 1¼ × 2¾ in)
0.27 kg (½ lb)

Plastic, metal
DM 195

The latest iteration in Braun's camera flash series, the F 200, swapped horizontal orientation for vertical, enabling easier access to the camera's controls. What was seemingly a simple decision created a new standard for the photography industry. The F 200 would inspire numerous future models, each one featuring the same basic design but with minor technical improvements.

Also in the series: F 260 (1965), F 270 (1966), F 110 and F 210 (1968), F 220, F 280 and F 290 (1969)

L 1000, 1965
Floor-standing loudspeaker with stand
Dieter Rams
Braun

117 × 75 × 33 cm (46 × 29½ × 13 in)
60 kg (132¼ lb)

Laminated wood, metal;
wire or metal grille
DM 3,500

To complement Braun's growing collection of high-end audio separates, Rams designed a range of equally high-end loudspeakers, intended to fill substantially sized rooms with superb quality sound. The numerous drivers integrated into this particular studio monitor, the L 1000, were housed in a tall box-like enclosure with a chamfered top edge. This could then be suspended on a matching stand, allowing the direction of the sound to be adjusted depending on the space. For the ultimate sound experience, Braun employed dynamic ribbon technology (also known as 'Kelly ribbons') across the series, which Rams paired with wire mesh or perforated aluminium grilles.

The L 1000 was preceded by two smaller models featuring the same design from 1962 and 1965; only 200 units of the L 1000 were produced in total.

Also in the series: L 80 (1962), L 700 (1965), L 800 and L 900 (1966)

PS 400, 1965 / PS 430, 1971 (pictured)
Record player
Dieter Rams
Braun

17.2 × 43 × 32 cm (6¾ × 17 × 13 in)
9.4 kg (20¾ lb)

Sheet steel, aluminium, acrylic, rubber
DM 478

This free-standing record player was extracted from the audio 2 system (p. 121). The slightly flattened plinth is in keeping with its predecessor, the PCS 5 of 1962 (p. 89), although the switches now slide instead of rotate. As a standalone unit, Braun manufactured 4,500 PS 400 devices.

Also in the series: PS 402 (1967), PS 410 (1968), PS 420 (1969)

PS 1000, 1965
Record player
Dieter Rams
Braun

17 × 42.8 × 31.7 cm (6¾ × 17 × 12½ in)
18 kg (40 lb)

Sheet steel, aluminium, plastic, acrylic
DM 1,900

In order to be suitable for Braun's 1000 series sound system (pp. 130–1), the accompanying record player also needed to be of the highest quality. First presented at the Internationale Stuttgarter Funkausstellung (International Radio Exhibition) in 1965, the PS 1000 was slightly wider than preceding models and featured a very hi-tech tonearm and pared-down controls. Braun produced a total of 1,900 units. A follow-up model, the PS 1000 AS, was further equipped with an anti-skating system. As with the series' amplifier, the later PS 500 model (p. 152) was only half the price, although technically superior.

Also in the series: PS 1000 AS (1965)

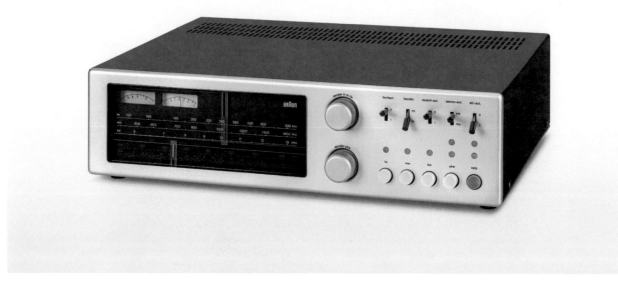

CE 1000, 1965
Tuner
Dieter Rams
Braun

10.5 × 40 × 33.5 cm (4 × 15¾ × 13 in)
10 kg (22 lb)

Sheet steel, aluminium, plastic, acrylic
DM 2,200

In terms of design, material and
technology, the tuner for Rams's 1000
high-end sound system took its lead
from the CSV 1000 amplifier (opposite);
however, it also featured elements that
informed Braun's later regie hi-fi series
(p. 153). The CE 1000 tuner was
produced in a small run of 800 units.

Also in the series: CE 1000-2 (1968)

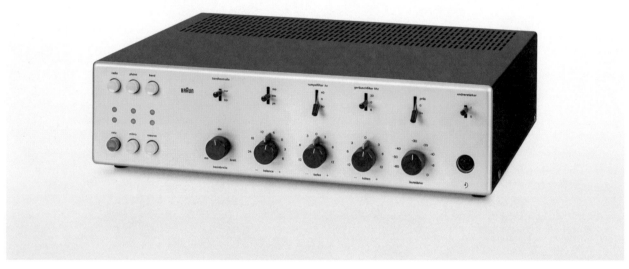

CSV 1000, 1965
Amplifier
Dieter Rams
Braun

10.5 × 40 × 33.5 cm (4 × 15¾ × 13 in)
14 kg (31 lb)

Sheet steel, aluminium, plastic
DM 2,400

In the mid-1960s, Braun entered the market for high-end audio equipment. The technology put into its 1000 series of audio devices was practically unrivalled in Germany – and Rams developed a design to match. The horizontal box shape was retained from the preceding CSV models, but the front panel was now covered with lacquered instead of anodized aluminium, which formed a perfect surface, with no visible screws. The controls include a series of delicate toggle switches along the top row and rotary switches below, some with an additional lever for adjusting the left or right channel. On the left side, there are six concave push buttons whose status is indicated by six corresponding LEDs. All these elements combine to form an extraordinary three-dimensional composition. However, technical and creative excellence also comes at a price; the complete system, including the Braun's L 1000 loudspeakers (p. 127), cost 13,500 deutschmarks; a base model Mercedes could be purchased for 10,800 marks at the time. As a result, only 1,100 units of this amplifier were produced, including its reworked successor, the CSV 1000-1 from 1968. The smaller CSV 500 variant, despite costing only half as much, was technically superior. Nevertheless, Braun discontinued its loss-making high-end segment in 1970.

Also in the series: CSV 500 (1967), CSV 1000-1 (1968)

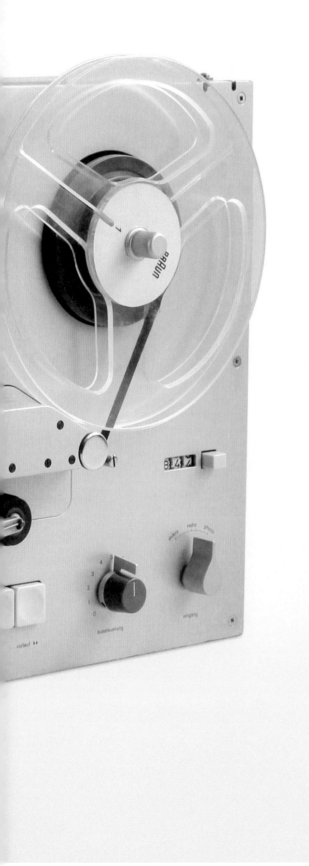

TG 60, 1965
Reel-to-reel tape recorder
Dieter Rams
Braun

28.3 × 42 × 13.5 cm (11 × 16½ × 5¼ in)
18.5 kg (40¾ lb)

Sheet steel, aluminium, plastic, acrylic
DM 1,980

Although tape recorders became
popular in the early 1960s, only
relatively simple equipment was
initially available for home use. This
presented Braun with a new technical
challenge if it was to serve the growing
market. Of all the Braun devices of the
time, the TG 60 is perhaps the one
that gives the greatest impression of
technology; the exposed tape reels
and tension arm, the teardrop-shaped
rotary switches and the prominent
control wheel for input signal levels
all contribute to its hi-tech appearance.
Designed for both domestic and
semi-professional environments, the
reel-to-reel device could be connected
to other Braun hi-fi modules, such as
its wall-mounted sound system
(pp. 98–9). The visual characteristics
of Rams's hi-fi separates seem largely
defined by this relationship between
the individual qualities of each unit and
the harmony they create when used
together. The TG 60 was produced in
a small run of 1,500 units.

Also in the series: TG 502 and TG 502-4
(1967), TG 550 (1968)

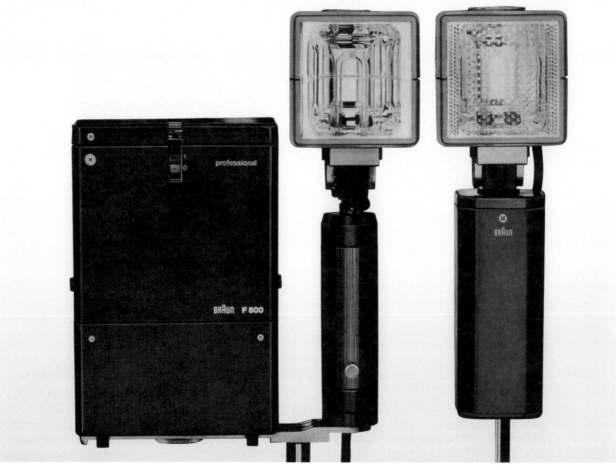

F 800 professional, 1965
Electronic camera flash
Dieter Rams
Braun

Power unit: 20.5 × 13.7 × 5.8 cm
(8 × 5½ × 2¼ in)
1.8 kg (4 lb)

Plastic, aluminium
DM 480–598

The F 800 was designed for
professional photojournalism. It
featured two flash bulbs on separate
holders, one with a diffuser and
one with clear glass, which could
be used together or separately.
The design retained the basic form
of Braun's larger flash models.

Also in the series: F 700 professional
(1968)

Nizo S 8, 1965
Super-8 movie camera
Robert Oberheim
Braun Nizo

12.2 × 23 × 4.5 cm (4¾ × 9 × 1¾ in)
0.98 kg (2¼ lb)

Aluminium, metal, plastic
DM 1,080

Following the release of Rams and Richard Fischer's EA 1 electric movie camera in 1964 (p. 115), Robert Oberheim took over the development of the range, refining the basic narrow box shape into a number of different models. The Nizo S 8 was his first iteration; its combination of aluminium side panels, injection-moulded core and retractable handle became the standard for Braun movie cameras. Operation was highly intuitive, meaning the instruction manual was essentially superfluous.

F 1000, 1966
Studio lighting system
Dieter Rams
Braun

Power unit: 41.5 × 40.5 × 20.4 cm
(16¼ × 16 × 8 in)
25 kg (55 lb)

Sheet steel, aluminium, plastic
From DM 4,200

Braun's studio lighting system consisted of a large number of components that could be combined: generators, floor lamps, spotlights, reflector screens, softboxes, halogen lamps, barn doors, filter holders, softbox grid inserts, wide beam reflectors and foot-operated switches. Each generator could power up to four flash lamps. Reflecting the packaging of Rams's hi-fi separates, his designs for the F 1000 series were enclosed in graphite-coloured housing with a cracked faux-leather finish paired with anodized aluminium for the control panel surfaces. While this lighting system was considered successful in technical and creative terms, it was very expensive and an economically disastrous experiment with which to enter a new market.

PK 1000 and PV 1000, 1966
Cross-type antenna and adaptor for
the T 1000 world-band receiver
Dieter Rams

Due to its capabilities as a navigational
instrument on boats, the T 1000
world-band receiver (p. 106) became
a popular choice for sailors; Braun
developed a cross-type antenna and
a corresponding adaptor as optional
accessories. Both devices were
produced in a run of 1,000 units.

Braun
PK 1000: 38.5 × 25 × 25 cm (15 × 9¾ ×
9¾ in); PV 1000: 5.5 × 9 × 9.5 cm
(2 × 3½ × 9¾ in)

PK 1000: 1.5 kg (3¼ lb); PV 1000:
0.25 kg (½ lb)
Metal, plastic, glass
PK 1000: DM 235; PV 1000: DM 245

CSV 250, 1966 (pictured with the
CE 250, 1967)
Amplifier
Dieter Rams

Braun
11 × 26 × 33.5 cm (4¼ × 10¼ × 13¼ in)
8 kg (17½ lb)

Sheet steel, aluminium, plastic
DM 698

As with its tuner counterpart
(opposite), the CSV 250 amplifier
was only a third of the price of
its 1000 series predecessor from
the previous year (p. 131). Designed
simultaneously, the two devices
featured only the essentials;
the controls were pared down to a
minimum and, with the exception
of the teardrop-shaped rotary switch,
the visual language comprised only
circles and rectangles.

Also in the series: CSV 250-1 (1969),
CSV 300 (1970)

CE 500, 1966
Tuner
Dieter Rams
Braun

Although cheaper than the
CE 1000 model (p. 130), the CE 500
maintained a level of performance
that was practically unchanged from
its predecessor, and its design was
considerably more compact. Erwin
Braun's 'Grand Design' concept was
now available for less than 1,000
deutschmarks.

Also in the series: CE 500 K (1966),
CE 250 (1967), CE 501, CE 501-1 and
CE 501 K (1969)

11 × 26 × 33.5 cm (4¼ × 10¼ × 13 in)
6.5 kg (14¼ lb)

Sheet steel, aluminium, plastic
DM 995

FS 600, 1966
Black-and-white television set
Dieter Rams
Braun

51 × 74.2 × 36 cm (20 × 29¼ × 14¼ in)
32 kg (70½ lb)

Laminated or veneered particle board
DM 995

Although this television was initially designed to transmit black-and-white images, it was also compatible with colour technology, requiring only minor design modifications to produce Braun's first colour set the following year. The enclosure was made of lacquered wood, from which the picture screen protrudes slightly, as was the case with preceding models. The setting and channel switches, and both VHF and UHF tuning scales, are aligned together in a grid in the lower half of the side control panel, while Braun's familiarly striking speaker grille occupies the upper half. A total of 2,500 units of the FS 600 television were produced.

Prototype enclosure for the HM 107
oscilloscope, c.1966
Dieter Rams
Braun / Hameg

20.7 × 15 × 24 cm (8 × 6 × 9½ in)
Weight unknown

Materials unknown
Not released for sale

To accompany Braun's ELA sound
system (pp. 143–4), Rams created
this beautifully shaped enclosure for
an oscilloscope, adopting design
elements from existing hi-fi equipment.
The device itself, which measures and
displays the voltage of an electrical
signal over time, was the HM 107,
produced by Hameg in Frankfurt in
1963, a company that specialized in
laboratory-grade instruments.
Whether it was intended exclusively
for technicians to use when servicing
the ELA system, or to be generally
available to all Braun repair shops,
is unknown. The prototype shown
here has not survived.

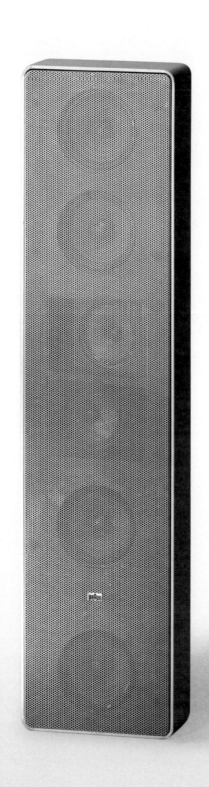

LS 75, 1965
Loudspeakers for the ELA system
Dieter Rams
Braun

These large-scale loudspeakers were designed prior to Braun's ELA system (below and overleaf), but ended up being incorporated into the series. The design is derived from Braun's smaller box-like speaker enclosures with pressed aluminium mesh grilles. Braun produced 600 units of the LS 75.

Also in the series: ELR 1 (1968)

98 × 40 × 14 cm (38½ × 15¾ × 5½ in)
17.5 kg (38½ lb)

Wood, anodized aluminium
DM 880
Pictured: opposite

ELA system, 1967–70
Public address (PA) system
Dieter Rams
Braun

89.1/173.6 × 60 × 46 cm (35/68½ × 23½ × 18 in)
Various weights

Sheet steel, aluminium
From DM 1,600
Pictured: overleaf

In 1967, Braun embarked on an ambitious new project in an attempt to establish itself in the market for professional PA systems. Intended for use in large spaces, such as churches, lecture halls, dance studios and nightclubs, the ELA (electro-acoustic transmission) system was made up of a series of existing Braun hi-fi devices that had been redesigned with matching front panels and were then inserted into large tower racks. The impetus for the project came after Braun's sales reps noticed a rise in the number of the company's electrostatic loudspeakers being bought by night-clubs, and so saw an opportunity to expand their customer base. However, they soon found that domestic hi-fi equipment was not suitable for continuous operation and the company's significant investment in the ELA system ended in financial failure. According to Rams, the project was carried out too half-heartedly.

Stand for a sound system and a
television set, 1967
Dieter Rams
Braun

Various sizes and weights

Die-cast aluminium, lacquered wood
From DM 55

Rams designed this cantilever stand
system to hold Braun's audio 1 and 2
sound systems, as well as other hi-fi
devices and the FS 1000 television
set (p. 146). Featuring a pair of slim skid
legs, or 'kangaroo feet', the cantilever
stands have a very lightweight appearance, giving the impression that
whatever is placed on them is floating.
Rams used this same construction
principle when designing a set
of folding chairs for Vitsoe+Zapf
(pp. 90–1) and the stand for the L 710
loudspeaker (p. 160) – yet another
example of his ability to create design
elements that could be seamlessly
transferred across products.

FS 1000, 1967
Colour television set
Dieter Rams
Braun

51 × 78 × 56 cm (20 × 30¾ × 22 in)
35 kg (77¼ lb)

Laminated particle board, plastic, glass
DM 2,580

Germany was introduced to the world of colour television at the opening of the twenty-fifth Große Deutsche Funk-Ausstellung (Great German Radio Exhibition) in Berlin in 1967. Initially, however, the German PAL system (standing for 'Phase Alternating Line', a colour-encoding system for analogue television) was only used for certain programmes. Braun anticipated this opportunity and came prepared with its FS 1000 colour TV, which was considerably more expensive than others on the market. The mail-order company Neckermann offered a set for 1,840 deutschmarks, while the Braun set cost almost 1,000 marks more. Consequently, Braun discontinued the device after producing only 1,000 units across two models. In terms of design, Rams adopted the same basic layout as the FS 600 (p. 140), but refined the arrangement of the control panel. The push-button switches and tuning scale were moved to their own indented section on the right and arranged in a single line, while the speaker grille slots were shortened and placed on the left. While the appearance of the FS 1000 was impressive, there was nothing special to distinguish it from the previous black-and-white model. The television set was designed as part of Braun's 1000 series of electronics, with the intention of integrating it into a complete home entertainment system made up of an amplifier, tuner and record player, all displayed together on a cantilever stand (p. 145).

Also in the series: FS 1010 (1969)

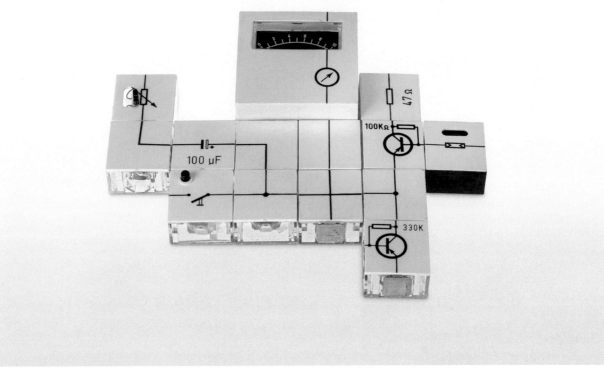

Lectron Minisystem, 1967
Electronic building blocks
Dieter Rams, Jürgen Greubel, Dietrich
Lubs, Georg Franz Greger

Braun
Single block: 1.6 × 2.7 × 2.7 cm
(½ × 1 × 1 in)
0.01 kg (½ oz)

Plastic, acrylic
From DM 58

On 7 May 1965, Georg Franz Greger filed a patent application for a system in which a series of magnetic blocks containing different electronic components could be freely arranged on a conductive plate to form a series of functional circuits. It was intended as an educational toy for children and young people, and for use in physics lessons at schools. Although the system was originally produced by the Egger-Bahn company, Braun took over the worldwide sales rights (excluding the United States) in 1967 and set about reworking the design. Braun later published an educational book, *Braun Buchlabor* (*Braun Book Lab*), which explained the various uses of the product, and also developed the

Schülerübungssysteme (School System), a more comprehensive and complex set of blocks for use by older students. The system was manufactured by Deutsche Lectron in Munich until 1972, after which it transferred to Lectron – a company founded by Braun engineer Manfred Walter in Frankfurt. Since 2011, the system has been manufactured by Reha Werkstatt in Frankfurt, a company that provides employment for those with learning disabilities.

T 2 cylindric, 1967
Prototype for a table lighter
Dieter Rams
Braun

7.3 × 5.1 cm in diameter (3 × 2 in)
0.4 kg (1 lb)

Stainless steel, plastic
Not released for sale

Following the release of Braun's first table lighter, the rectangular TFG 1, designed by Reinhold Weiss in 1966, Rams created a cylindrical model that would go on to become very successful. Even in this preliminary prototype, it is possible to see the design's now-familiar shape developing. In contrast to the fully realized design, however, the prototype is rather squat and the ignition button sits on the top. This first iteration followed the traditional form of a lighter, where a user's four fingers grip the body while the thumb presses the ignition on the top. However, this construction placed the thumb too close to the flame, and made using the large device a somewhat clumsy operation. The final shape of the T 2 cylindric resulted in a completely different grip, determined by the oversized concave ignition button, now positioned on the side of the lighter (opposite).

T 2 cylindric, 1968
Table lighter
Dieter Rams
Braun

8.8 × 5.4 cm in diameter (3½ × 2 in)
Metal: 0.25 kg (8¾ oz); plastic: 0.17 kg
(6 oz)

Metal, plastic or leather
DM 75–168

In the mid-1960s, smoking was considered an acceptable social activity. It was also common practice for a gentleman to offer to light a woman's cigarette. This gesture led to the design of a product that differed from the ostentatious jewellery-inspired lighters of the past, and instead sought to combine functionality with value. Similar to the way in which Reinhold Weiss chose a standing cuboid form, incorporated from his 1961 HT 1 toaster design, to create his first lighter, Rams adopted a basic geometric shape for the T 2, using, in this case, an elongated cylinder and devising all the details exclusively in circular forms. The design combines pure elegance and clean lines with maximum functionality; it can be easily operated with one hand, allowing its ergonomic form to be enjoyed. The result was practical 'table sculpture' that reflected the Minimalist art trend of the time. This successful model, which originally used magnetic ignition technology and later piezo ignition, appeared in numerous finishes, ranging from luxury silver plating to a fluted chrome version, as well as an array of plastic options in the block colours of contemporary Pop art. By the late 2000s, there were several imitations of the cylindric lighter being produced by external companies under the brand names Cozy Berlin, Colibri and Berlin II, the last of these having two flame jets.

Also in the series: TFG 2 cylindric (1968)

680, 1968
Sofa bed programme
Dieter Rams
Vitsœ+Zapf / Vitsœ

38 × 204 × 89–159 cm (15 × 80¼ ×
35–62½ in)
approx. 40 kg (88¼ lb)

Polystyrene foam, polyurethane foam;
fabric or leather upholstery
DM 743–2,580

This sofa bed seems to be made
almost entirely from one solid form.
It has a very low frame with two
longitudinal, two transverse and four
corner sections made of polystyrene
foam, which can be easily dismantled
and stored underneath for transport.
The mattress consists of a large,
thermally insulating polystyrene core
with grooves and cavities for air
circulation, on top of which is a block
of 13-cm (5-in) -thick polyurethane
foam; it can be upholstered in a variety
of different fabrics, or leather. The
sofa bed's natural monolithic shape,
with its cleverly designed inner
structure, allows it to be positioned
in many parts of the home without
overpowering its surroundings.

681, 1968
Chair programme
Dieter Rams
Vitsoe+Zapf / Vitsœ

61 × 79 × 75 cm (24 × 31 × 29½ in)
13 kg (28¾ lb)

Polystyrene foam, polyurethane foam;
Dacron, fabric or leather upholstery
DM 2,795 (price from 1980)

To accompany the 680 sofa bed
(opposite), Rams created a matching
chair. It followed the same design and
construction principles, allowing the
chair's backrest to be mounted onto
the sofa bed to create a lounger. With
the addition of a steel connecting
bracket, individual armchairs could
also be combined to form a sofa,
demonstrating how the system-based
approach was prominent in every
aspect of Rams's design practice.

PS 500, 1968
Record player
Dieter Rams
Braun

17 × 43 × 32 cm (6¾ × 17 × 13 in)
12.6 kg (27¾ lb)

Wood, sheet steel, plastic, acrylic
DM 750

The PS 500 is one of Braun's most sophisticated record players, for which Rams chose a very clean geometric form. The platter is suspended on a solid zinc, injection-moulded sub-chassis with hydraulic damping. Moreover, the construction of the belt drive is complex and very precise, and the tonearm features an anti-skating guide. When in use, the PS 500's pulsating stroboscope display with its deep red light gives the impression that the device is alive. An impressive 44,000 units of the record player were produced.

Also in the series: PS 500 E (1968), PSQ 500 (1973)

regie 500, 1968
Stereo receiver
Dieter Rams
Braun

11 × 40 × 32 cm (4¼ × 15¾ × 12½ in)
14 kg (31 lb)

Sheet steel, aluminium, plastic, acrylic
DM 1,895

In 1968, Rams designed a new class of hi-fi audio equipment, which took the form of a compact receiver, combining a radio with a power amplifier. Based on the flat rectangular box design of the studio 2 product line (p. 53) and the high-end 1000 series (p. 130), the regie 500 featured a graphite-coloured casing and an aluminium front panel on which all display and control elements were arranged. Rams used concave push-button switches and dual-functioning rotary knobs; the front is smooth without visible screws.

This was one of the rare occasions that a product was given a name beyond Braun's traditional letter and number combinations. A total of nineteen regie

models were released in the years that followed, and 180,000 units produced.

Also in the series: regie 501 and regie 501 K (1969)

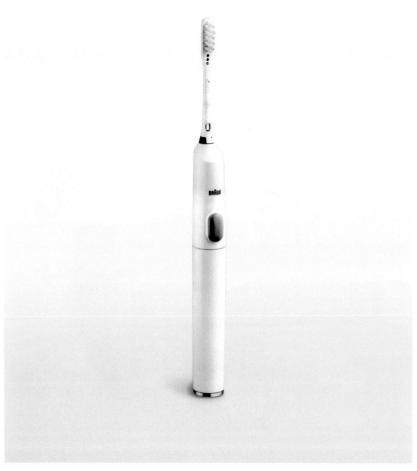

Prototype for an electric toothbrush, 1968
Dieter Rams
Braun

Size and weight unknown

Plastic, metal
Not released for sale

This prototype for an electric toothbrush was found in Rams's patent application archive, and has never before been published. The design was produced only five years after Mayadent's first electric toothbrush was released in 1963 – created by Willi Zimmermann, advertising manager of Braun's Swiss subsidiary. However, it predates Braun's regular production of electric toothbrushes by almost a decade. Rams's design is extraordinarily elegant and much slimmer than that of later versions; its long oval button mimics that used on the T 2 cylindric lighter (p. 149). Unfortunately, the model was never produced. The text in the Soviet patent reads: 'Industrial Design Patent No. 894, issued by the Committee for Inventions and Discoveries at the Council of Ministers of the USSR for the foreign company Braun Corporation, Federal Republic of Germany, for the industrial design of a toothbrush with electric motor and a brush to be inserted into the handle. Author of the industrial design: Dieter Rams. The patent is valid in the entire territory of the USSR for five years starting on 13 February 1969. Moscow, 20 November 1969.'

Although it is not known why the toothbrush never made it to production, previous negotiations between Braun and Soviet state-run companies to enter the market for shaver production in the USSR had failed. Erwin Braun's offer to deliver semi-finished goods for assembly in the Soviet Union, which would have prevented the transfer of technical knowledge, were rejected by the state. This may have been the reason why the new product was patented in the country.

HW 1, 1968
Bathroom scales
Dieter Rams, Dietrich Lubs
Braun

27 × 31 × 6.5 cm (10½ × 5 × 2½ in)
4 kg (8¾ lb)

Metal, plastic, acrylic
DM 34.50

The special feature of these bathroom scales is an analogue measuring device that allows individual family members to record their weight. This simple 'memory scale' was a novelty; a thin steel rod extends along the top of the scales and holds a set of coloured plastic rings that can be moved along the rail and placed according to the weight measurements marked on a ruler below. The HW 1 scales also feature all the recognizable Braun design elements, such as the combination of black plastic and metal, and the precision typography of the scale display with magnifying window.

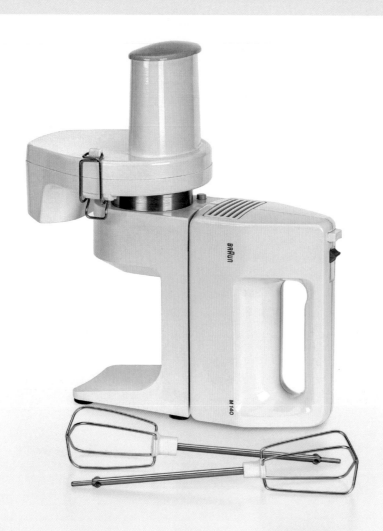

M 140 Multiquirl, with MS 140
shredder, MZ 140 citrus juicer and MZ
142 electric knife attachments, 1968
Hand mixer and attachments

Reinhold Weiss, Dieter Rams
Braun
17.5 × 13/28.5 × 7.5 cm (7 × 5/11¼ × 3 in)
1.06 kg (2¼ lb)

Plastic
DM 20–59

The M 140 hand mixer by Reinhold
Weiss, based on a design that he
originally created with Hans Gugelot
at the HfG Ulm, was given a small but
decisive adjustment by Rams to
enhance its ease of use: an indentation
in the handle for the index finger,
providing a much firmer grip. Rams
applied the same feature to a series
of door handle designs he produced
in the 1980s for manufacturer FSB
(pp. 312–14). The Multiquirl's standard
whisk attachment could be adapted
with a gearbox, transforming the hand
mixer into a mini food processor with
shredder, electric knife and citrus
juicer attachments.

KMM 2, 1969
Coffee grinder
Dieter Rams
Braun

18.9 × 11.5 × 8.2–12 cm in diameter
(7½ × 4½ × 3¼–4¾ in)
0.95 kg (2 lb)

Plastic, acrylic
DM 49.50

The grinding mechanism in this design is located between an upper storage/dispensing unit for the coffee beans and a lower container that collects the ready-to-use ground coffee. The result is a tower-like construction, the principle of which was later used in Florian Seiffert's KF 20 coffee machine from 1972 (pp. 190–1). The relatively large container at the top allowed for a greater volume of coffee beans, while the flattening of the two sides of the lower section meant the grinder could be easily gripped with one hand. One of Braun's strengths as a design company was its ability to transfer established forms, which had already proven their practical or aesthetic value, into other devices. The window displaying the amount of ground coffee, for example, is the same shape as the ignition button of the T 2 table lighter (p. 149); and the rocker switch at the base of the coffee grinder would later be applied to the HLD 4 hair dryer of 1970 (pp. 172–3). This natural continuity between products demonstrates a tried-and-tested thought process that defined Rams's design approach – although it never became a dogma.

690, 1969
Sliding door system
Dieter Rams
Vitsoe+Zapf / Vitsœ

Various sizes and weights
Extruded polystyrene, aluminium, wood

Doors and framework: DM 1,125; slats:
DM 265 (prices from 1983)

This sliding door system meant wall niches could be turned into built-in cupboards, or an entire room could be divided. The supporting structure consists of vertical aluminium pillars that are clamped between floor and ceiling, with guide rails installed at the top and bottom. The light grey sliding doors are made up of flexible, vertical slats of extruded polystyrene, fixed in place using tongue-and-groove joints. The top and bottom sections of the structure are the same shape as the base components of Rams's 680 sofa bed programme (p. 150). Theoretically, the system was endlessly expandable. Its basic frame was modelled on the vertical profiles used in Vitsœ's 606 Universal Shelving System (pp. 65–9), which was then supplemented with running and guiding tracks.

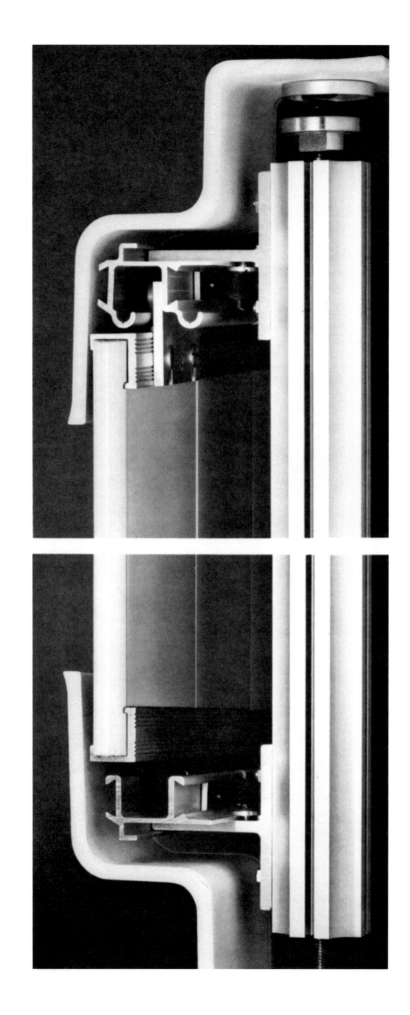

L 710, 1969
Studio loudspeaker with stand
Dieter Rams
Braun

55 × 31 × 24 cm (21¾ × 12¼ × 9½ in)
18 kg (39¾ lb)

Laminated wood, steel, anodized
aluminium
DM 595

This loudspeaker, created with audio technician Franz Petrik, was very successful for Braun, with more than 100,000 units manufactured across the entire series. Compared to other speakers in its price range, the neutral sound it produced was outstanding. The L 710 could also be distinguished from its predecessors by its gently rounded corners; this small but decisive change resulted in a harmonious enclosure design, which complemented the appearance of Braun's other hi-fi separates of the day, such as the regie 500 (p. 153). The elegant form of the loudspeaker could be enhanced by the addition of a pair of skid legs (named LF 700), which were sold separately and allowed the speaker to be raised off the floor and tilted gracefully at an angle to the room.

Also in the series: L 810 (1969), L 710-1 (1973), L 715 (1975)

L 610, 1969 / L 500, 1970 (pictured)
Bookshelf loudspeaker
Dieter Rams
Braun

Braun's L 500 / L 600 series of
loudspeakers were a smaller version
of the L 710 (opposite). Containing
two or three drivers, the loudspeaker
enclosure is largely identical in design
to that of the larger models, but has
slightly different proportions.

Also in the series: L 620 (1971), L 500-1
(1973), L 625 (1974)

45 × 25 × 22 cm (17¾ × 9¾ × 8¾ in)
9.5 kg (21 lb)

Laminated wood, anodized aluminium
DM 460

1970–1979

Prototype for a torch, 1970
Dieter Rams
Braun

11 × 4 × 2.8 cm (4¼ × 1½ × 1 in)
0.12 kg (¼ lb)

Plastic, acrylic
Not released for sale

This battery-operated torch has a
cylindrical shape and an angled bulb
compartment, meaning that it could
be held upright, resulting in a more
comfortable interaction. Although the
design was ergonomically sound, it
did not make it into production.

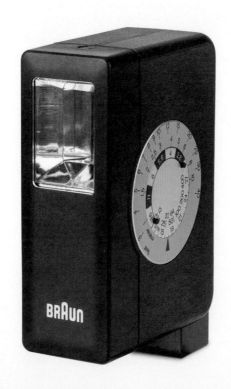

F 240 LS hobby-mat, 1970 /
F 111 hobby, 1971 (pictured)
Electronic camera flash
Dieter Rams

Braun
9.5 × 6.3 × 3 cm (3¾ × 2½ × 1¼ in)
0.2 kg (½ lb)

Plastic, metal
DM 129 (F 111 hobby)

Here, Braun's standard flash model, established with the F 200 (p. 126), is reproduced in all-black, reflecting the packaging of the company's hi-fi audio components of the time, as well as the industry's mostly black SLR cameras. The colour was also a practical choice as it helped to avoid reflections. The flash's front panel protrudes at a 45-degree angle from the frame, adding another level of three-dimensionality to the design. All the devices in this series were manufactured in Japan.

Also in the series: F 410 LS hobby-mat (1970), F 16 B hobby, F 245 LSR and F 18 LS hobby-mat (1971), F 17 hobby (1972)

Prototype for an accessory
loudspeaker, 1970
Dieter Rams
Braun

29 × 14 × 17 cm (11½ × 5½ × 6¾ in)
0.5 kg (1 lb)

Plastic
Not released for sale

This prototype for a slim loudspeaker
was designed to accompany the
T 2002 world-band receiver (opposite).
The curved enclosure featured large
holes in its speaker grille, which were
later worked into the speakers for the
cockpit hi-fi series (p. 186).

T 2002, 1970
Prototype for a world-band receiver
Dieter Rams
Braun

29 × 37.5 × 17 cm (11½ × 14¾ × 6¾ in)
1 kg (2¼ lb)

Plastic
Not released for sale

In the age of plastic, it was only fitting that the successor to the T 1000 world-band receiver (p. 106) should be upgraded to reflect the material of the moment. Rams's reworking of the iconic model did not sacrifice its distinctiveness of form, but, when closed, the device now had the appearance of a white box. Inside, a striking black interface appears, upon which all the controls are arranged in a strict geometric grid. The aesthetics of the device are strongly defined by this contrast between white casing and black interior. The tuning scales were protected by a panel of transparent acrylic, a feature that would later be applied to the regie hi-fi series; the same series conversely influenced the use of black in the T 2002 control panel, which was intended to reflect the cutting-edge technology of the regie sound systems.

In addition to its function as a world-band receiver, the T 2002 was intended for use as a small stationary sound system, with two specially designed loudspeakers created for this purpose (opposite). The small, built-in 'listening speaker' was only meant for short-wave news broadcasts, otherwise headphones would mostly have been used.

TG 1000, 1970
Reel-to-reel tape recorder
Dieter Rams
Braun

32 × 45 × 12.5 cm (12½ × 17¾ × 5 in)
17 kg (37½ lb)

Sheet steel, plastic, aluminium
DM 1,798

Following the debut of the TG 60 in 1965 (pp. 132–3), Braun's second generation of reel-to-reel tape recorders was the perfect match for both the high-end modular devices developed in the second half of the 1960s and the newer regie sound systems of the 1970s (p. 187). In terms of technology, this semi-professional device was superior to almost all competing German products. The all-metal control panel features a clear arrangement of switches, level meters and DIN sockets across three horizontal rows. The power button is green, the record button is red and all others are white or grey. The transport buttons for start, stop, fast forward and rewind functions make a rich crackling noise when in operation, and although the rewinding speed is impressively fast, it can be stopped swiftly by a highly effective electromechanical braking system. All of these elements combine to provide the user with a unique visual, haptic and acoustic experience. The TG 1000 tape recorders were first manufactured by Braun in Kronberg, with a total of 28,000 units produced, but the TG 1020 and subsequent models were produced by contract manufacturer Uher in Munich.

Also in the series: TG 1000-2 (1970), TG 1000-4 (1972), TG 1020 and TG 1020-4 (1974)

cockpit 250 S, 1970
Radio-record player combination
Dieter Rams
Braun

18 × 57 × 34 cm (7 × 22½ × 13½ in)
14 kg (31 lb)

Plastic, acrylic
DM 1,298

The cockpit combined radio and
record player offered an inexpensive
alternative to Braun's 'audio' series
sound system (pp. 88 and 121).
First presented at the Deutsche Funk-
ausstellung (German Radio Exhibition)
in Düsseldorf in 1970, its target market
was the younger generation, and it
was the first of Braun's audio products
to feature an all-plastic casing. Due
to the limitations of the production
process, the plinth was tapered for
easy removal from the mould.
Approximately 16,000 units of each
cockpit model were produced.

Also in the series: 250 SK (1970), 250
W and 250 WK (1970–1), 260 S and
260 SK (1972)

T 3, 1970
Table lighter
Dieter Rams
Braun

5.5 × 5.5 × 6 cm (2¼ × 2¼ × 2½ in)
0.13 kg (¼ lb)

Plastic, metal
DM 50

This lighter design represents the transformation of a cube into an aesthetically refined object. The asymmetrical rounding of the corners affects both its look and feel; the shadow gap above the base makes the lighter appear to float; and the combination of circle and dot forms serves as both an indicator of function and a pleasing design feature. Furthermore, the black dot on the side of the lighter ties in visually with the black border surrounding the flame opening.

While the T 3 was fitted with an electric ignition operated by a 15-volt battery, Braun's follow-up model, the domino, used cheaper piezo technology. As a result, the button on the later model

protrudes slightly from the surface (p. 225), and requires the user to push down harder to ignite. In a lighter, piezoelectric technology operates via a spring-loaded hammer that strikes a crystal when the button is pressed, creating an electric charge. This is what causes the typical 'clicking' sound a lighter makes when used.

Also in the series: domino (1976)

D 300, 1970
Slide projector
Robert Oberheim
Braun

22 × 25.2 × 12 cm (8¾ × 10 × 4¾ in)
4.3 kg (9½ lb)

Plastic
DM 329

Taking its lead from the D 50 prototype designed by Rams in 1958 (p. 47), this compact slide projector features a distinctive opening underneath the light where the slide tray was positioned – although this time, the industry-standard Leitz tray system was used, rather than Braun's own. The D 300 was placed on an adjustable stand, allowing the user to change the angle of the projection beam; it could also be mounted on a tripod. Designer Robert Oberheim drew inspiration from other Braun devices when choosing the shape of the control switches, which, through their elegant forms, double as design features.

Also in the series: D 300 autofocus (1974)

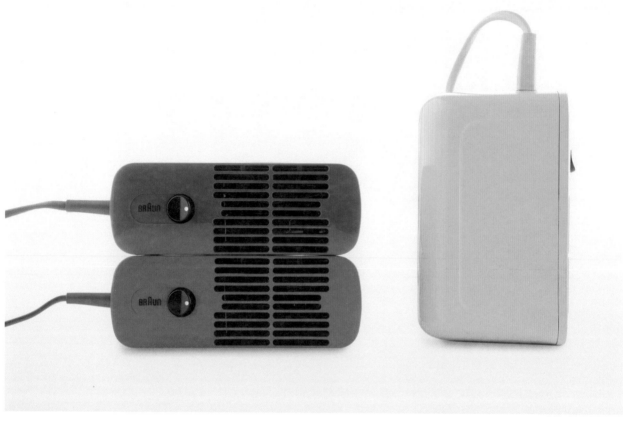

HLD 4, 1970
Travel hair dryer
Dieter Rams
Braun

5.4 × 14.1 × 9 cm (2 × 5½ × 3½ in)
0.24 kg (½ lb)

Plastic
DM 34.50

Using tangential blower technology,
Rams designed a completely new
form of hair dryer. The HLD 4, with its
distinctly rounded edges, came in the
primary colours of red, yellow and blue.
The device can be gripped easily from
the back, which was freed of any air
inlet slots that might accidentally be
covered by the user's hand. Instead,
the air inlet and outlet are both found
on the front. However, one side effect
of this construction was turbulence,
which resulted in a slightly weakened
airflow – although some people found
this to be a pleasant feature.

MP 50, 1970
Juice extractor
Jürgen Greubel
Braun

29 × 20 cm in diameter (11½ × 8 in)
3.7 kg (8¼ lb)

Plastic, metal
DM 169

It was not until 1970 that Gerd A
Müller's MP 3 juice extractor,
designed in 1957, was replaced
by a new device – and even then it
used more or less the same basic
technology. The cylindrical design
of the MP 50 is wider and more
voluminous than its predecessor
and the curved upper edge rounds
into a shallow recess at the top,
a form that is reflected in the base
where a concave indentation
provides space for the juice to be
collected. This latter feature could
also be seen in the citromatic MPZ
juicer from 1972 (pp. 189–90). A red
dot on the spout indicates where
a user should position their glass.

Prototype for a coffee grinder, 1970
Dieter Rams
Braun

28.8 × 13 × 12 cm (11¼ × 5 × 4¾ in)
1.5 kg (3¼ lb)

Plastic, acrylic
Not released for sale

Alongside a design for a coffee maker
(p. 176), Rams worked on an idea for
a wall-mounted grinder that could
be moved up and down on a vertical
track to allow different collecting
containers to be used. Its distinctive
design features a long oval window
that displays the level of beans in
the grinder, and push buttons that
echo those used on Braun's hi-fi
audio devices.

Prototype for a coffee maker, 1970
Dieter Rams, Jürgen Greubel
Braun

34 × 23 × 17 cm (13½ × 9 × 6¾ in)
3.75 kg (8¼ lb)

Plastic, acrylic
Not released for sale

Adopting the tower-style form first
established by Florian Seiffert in his
early designs for the KF 20 coffee
maker (pp. 190–1), Rams and Jürgen
Greubel created this beautifully
resolved prototype. The transparent
acrylic water reservoir sits at the top,
while the filter and jug are inserted
into the tower underneath. The bright
yellow compartment handles align
one above the other to form a striking
line down the front.

cassett, 1970
Travel shaver
Florian Seiffert
Braun

10 × 6 × 3.5 cm (4 × 2½ × 1½ in)
0.17 kg (½ lb)

Plastic
DM 54

This battery-operated travel shaver clearly differs from the more rounded designs of Braun's sixtant models. Its boxy shape tapers at the top, and the enclosure – which came in red, black or yellow – features a prominent round control switch in a contrasting colour. The device can be stowed in a partially open case for transport, a solution later adopted for Braun's first pocket calculators. The use of bright colours distinguished the cassett from Braun's domestic shaver range.

Also in the series: cassett standard (1972)

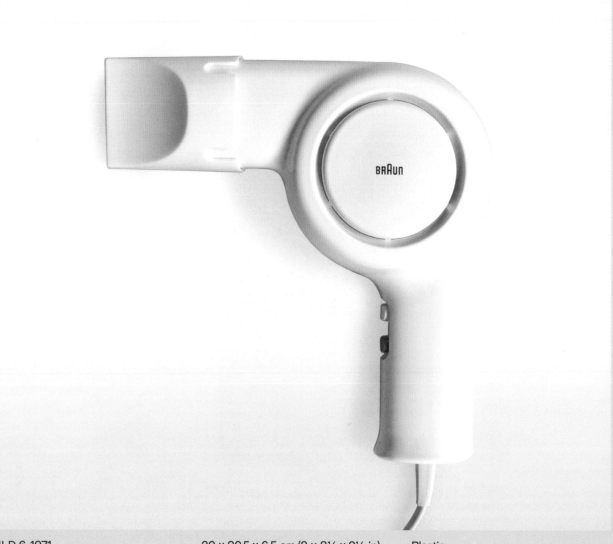

HLD 6, 1971
Hair dryer
Jürgen Greubel, Dieter Rams
Braun

20 × 20.5 × 6.5 cm (8 × 8¼ × 2½ in)
0.55 kg (1¼ lb)

Plastic
DM 39.50

This hair dryer comprises a rectangular handle and nozzle attached to a large round blower unit, whose shape is further emphasized by the circular interstice formed by the air intake slots. The vertical handle may have been chosen in an attempt to target professional hairdressers, for whom this was standard at the time. The resulting form is satisfyingly clean and geometric, and represents the successful transfer of a 1920s hair dryer design by Sanitas or AEG to the new plastic material.

Also in the series: HLD 61 (1971)

phase 1, 1971
Alarm clock
Dieter Rams, Dietrich Lubs
Braun

8 × 18 × 10 cm (3 × 7 × 4 in)
0.6 kg (1¼ lb)

Plastic, acrylic
DM 108–125

Flip clocks, those with split-flap displays such as the ones historically used at airports, had been appearing on the market since the mid-1960s, and mainly came from Japan. In 1971, Braun developed a similar device, but instead used a rotating display mechanism. The phase 1 alarm clock has a slightly slanted front panel in black that displays the time and the alarm setting. As with Rams's design for the T 2002 receiver (p. 167), as well as other Braun hi-fi devices, the use of black can be interpreted as representing technology and precision. The body of the clock, with its well-rounded edges, came in white, olive or red, the last of these colours a concession to the era's prevailing

fashion for Pop art. According to Dietrich Lubs, a collaborator on the design, they could not always influence the size and style of number fonts as the corresponding parts of the clock were sourced from external suppliers.

620, 1971
Chair/container programme
Dieter Rams
Vitsœ

38 × 66 × 66 cm (15 × 26 × 26 in)
approx. 20 kg (44 lb)

Plastic
DM 620

This unusual item of furniture serves
as a table, container or planter box for
indoor plants. The castors at the base
allow it to be moved around easily.
Originally designed in 1962, this piece
exemplifies Rams's understanding of
mobility and visual clarity in the home.

710, 1971
Container programme
Dieter Rams
Vitsœ / sdr+

Various sizes and weights

Laminated particle board
DM 278–1,048 (prices from 1973)

This furniture range was primarily
intended for use in offices, but
was also suitable for private homes.
The storage units can be used
individually or in combination with
one another. They consist of 19-mm
(¾-in) -thick, laminated wood panels,
with feet or castors at the base. For
this series, Rams again applied a
modular design approach, reflecting
the work he did fourteen years earlier
with the RZ 57 (p. 28).

Dieter and Ingeborg Rams private
residence, Kronberg, Germany, 1971
Dieter Rams

Dieter and Ingeborg Rams's private
home was another project that fell
within the designer's scope. In 1958,
Braun acquired the right of first refusal
for an area of land in the north of
Kronberg, at the edge of the Taunus
forest, in order to build a residential
estate for executives, with separate
houses for visitors. The Am Roten
Hang (on the red hillside) development
took its inspiration from the 1961 Halen
Estate in Bern, Switzerland, designed
by Swiss architecture firm Atelier 5.
Both sites featured a series of terraced
structures connected by footpaths on a
forested plot, and were largely car free.

Rams started producing the first
sketches for the buildings in July 1967;
however, that same year Braun was
bought by Gillette and the land was
sold back to the city. The project was
then taken over by the Königstein-
based architect Rudolf Kramer,
although he referred to Rams's
preliminary sketches in his own work.
Dieter and Ingeborg Rams acquired
a large plot on the northern edge of
the settlement on which they built a
semi-detached bungalow. In contrast
to the rest of the estate, the Rams
residence featured dark wooden
window frames and white floor tiles.
Rams based the design of his large
terraced garden with a swimming
pool on the Japanese styles that he
loved; he also designed the home's
interior and filled it mostly with his own
furniture. The layout of the house
has hardly changed since the couple
moved in at the end of 1971. Today
the entire estate has been listed
under heritage protection, and on
15 September 2016, the Rams home
was declared a cultural monument
by the State Conservation Office
of Hessen, preventing any changes
being made to it, either inside or
out – something the couple would
never consider doing anyway.

F 1 mactron, 1971
Pocket lighter
Dieter Rams
Braun

7 × 3.3 × 1.3 cm (2¾ × 1¼ × ½ in)
0.1 kg (¼ lb)

Plastic, die-cast zinc, chrome plating
DM 98

Between 1971 and 1981, Braun released a large number of pocket lighters whose manufacture was outsourced. Most of the models were designed by Rams himself, though a few others came out of the Gugelot Institute and Busse Design Ulm, another studio set up by a former student (Rido Busse) of the HfG Ulm. Rams's design for the first Braun pocket lighter, the F 1 mactron, took the form of a flattened and elongated block. Using the thumb, part of the casing can be opened to reveal the lighting mechanism. This process of operation was so novel that it was successfully patented in several countries in the designer's name. The lighter uses electromagnetic ignition and its refill valve opening is positioned on the side, a placement reminiscent of the fuel tank cover on a sports car. Requiring a special adaptor to refill, this extravagant design feature was later abandoned in favour of a conventional position on the underside; the design's successor, the linear, is identical aside from the position of the refill valve. Braun advertising described the F 1 as: 'Braun's top-of-the range lighter. Unique in form and material. A clear alternative to ornamental decoration, luxury finishes and impractical shapes.' The solid, die-cast zinc casing contributed to its high quality appeal, just as much as the tried and tested combination of shiny metal and black textured plastic.

Also in the series: linear (1976)

mach 2, 1971
Pocket lighter
Florian Seiffert, Dieter Rams
Braun

5.7 × 3 × 1.3 cm (2¼ × 1¼ × ½ in)
0.06 kg (2 oz)

Metal, plastic
DM 39

Rams played a small but decisive part in this lighter design by Florian Seiffert; he was responsible for the distinctive tail flick on the ignition button. This detail acts as a counterpoint to the otherwise strict rectangular shape and was a significant improvement in terms of ergonomics. The mach 2 used piezo technology and was manufactured by Nuremberg-based Gebrüder Köllisch AG, the makers of Consul lighters, which was made a subsidiary of Braun in 1971.

L 260, 1972
Shelf or wall-mounted loudspeakers
Dieter Rams
Braun

30 × 19 × 19 cm (11¾ × 7½ × 7½ in)
3.5 kg (7¾ lb)

Plastic
DM 248

Designed as an accompaniment to
the cockpit sound system (p. 169),
these inexpensive loudspeakers were
based on the prototype developed
for the T 2002 world-band receiver
(p. 166). The small disc at the front
displaying the Braun logo can be
rotated according to the orientation
of the speakers.

regie 510, 1972 / regie 520, 1974
(pictured)
Receiver
Dieter Rams

Braun
11.5 × 50 × 33.5 cm (4½ × 19¾ × 13 in)
15 kg (33 lb)

Sheet steel, lacquered aluminium,
plastic, acrylic
DM 1,750

For his regie 510 receiver from 1972, Rams chose an all-black facade, which was to become the benchmark colour for both Braun's own range and the audio industry as a whole over the next three decades. The construction of the receiver is similar to that of the regie 500 (p. 153), but the rectangular box shape is wider and incorporates an interface layout that is closer to the CE 1000 tuner of 1965 (p. 130). The device is clearly divided into two parts, with the amplifier on the left and the radio on the right, each with their respective controls; the tuning frequency is indicated by a thin red pointer.

After producing 35,000 units of the original 510 model, Braun expanded the regie series throughout 1975 and 1976, releasing numerous iterations, many of which were modified by other Braun engineers. In contrast to the high-end models, which were only available through authorized Braun retailers, lower-quality devices, such as the regie 350, were also sold through department stores at the insistence of the company's sales team. The CE 1020 receiver, designed in 1973, and identical in construction to the 510 model except for the removal of the amplifier section, was intended for use with Braun's CSQ 1020 quadrophonic preamplifier (p. 197). It had a wider tuning scale than the regie 510; however, as so few radio stations were making use of the new four-way

technology, this sound set-up was mostly used by radio companies for test broadcasts. Nevertheless, the CE 1020 was still excellently suited for normal stereo radio reception. On 1 January 1974, price-fixing was banned in Germany. This led to the dissolution of what had, until then, been an important relationship between Braun and its specialist audio retailers.

Also in the series: regie 450 (1975), regie 450 S and regie 350 (1976), regie 525, regie 526, regie 528 and regie 530 (1977)

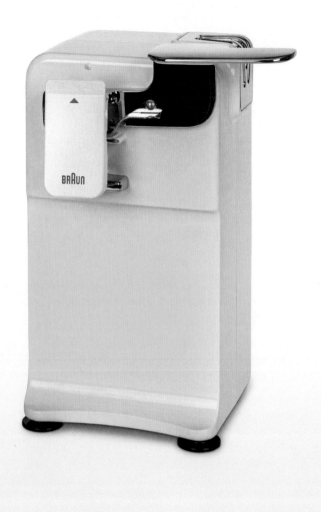

DS 1 Sesamat, 1972
Electric can opener
Dieter Rams, Jürgen Greubel,
Gabriel Lluelles

Braun Española
21 × 11.5 × 12 cm (8¼ × 4½ × 4¾ in)
2.1 kg (4½ lb)

Metal, plastic
Price unknown

This combined electric tin opener
and knife sharpener was produced by
Braun's Spanish subsidiary, primarily
for the local market, and sold under
the name Braun Abrematic. The heavy
device is propped up by plastic feet
and features a hinged protective cover
over the cutting mechanism to prevent
injury if accidentally switched on.

citromatic MPZ 2, 1972
Citrus juicer
Dieter Rams, Jürgen Greubel,
Gabriel Lluelles

In 1962, Braun acquired a Spanish household appliance manufacturer, Barcelona-based Pimer, and transformed it into Braun Española. The design process was still managed by Braun's Kronberg offices, but it was the responsibility of local design engineers, such as Gabriel Lluelles, to help in the development of products for the Spanish market. In fact, Lluelles had a hand in producing one of Braun's most successful kitchen appliances, the citromatic MPZ 2 juicer. The design was initially developed by Rams and Jürgen Greubel specifically for Braun Española, with the aim of targeting Spain's many small bars and cafes. However, when the juicer was first released it featured a lid design by

Braun Española
21.5 × 15 cm in diameter (8½ × 6 in)
1.3 kg (3 lb)

Lluelles, which, rather than following the natural contours of the juicing cone, had a more conventional flat surface. Rams recalled that it took a lot of persuasion and time to convince the Braun Española management to change the design. But eventually he and Greubel succeeded, and this extraordinary and beautifully shaped appliance – resembling a squat column with a flared Doric capital and dome – can still be found in many establishments today. The two design directions illustrate just how important seemingly simple details are for aesthetic quality, but equally for communicating a design's function; the pronounced spout and large juicing cone reveal precisely what

Plastic, acrylic
DM 51.50
Pictured: previous page

this machine is all about: freshly squeezed orange juice. Similar to the MP 50 juice extractor of 1970 (p. 174), the citromatic's cylindrical casing is recessed beneath the spout to securely accommodate a glass. To this day, the juicer is sold in its original design, under licence by De'Longhi, as the Braun Tribute Collection CJ 3050.

Also in the series: MPZ 21 (1994), MPZ 22 (1994)

KF 20, 1972
Coffee maker
Florian Seiffert
Braun

As a young member of Braun's design team, Florian Seiffert received some unconventional advice from Rams, who suggested he design a coffee maker that was 'more like a samovar than a chemical plant'. In contrast to the rather technical appearance of the day's coffee machines – an unappealing combination of tanks and tubes – Rams imagined something more sculptural. Seiffert's response was the KF 20, a design that was not only attractive but also innovative. Instead of placing the water reservoir next to the pot and filter, as was the norm, Seiffert opted for a tower-like arrangement, with the reservoir on top, supported by two crescent-shaped tubes, and the coffee pot underneath.

38.5 × 15 cm in diameter (15¼ × 6 in)
1.8 kg (4 lb)

However, this resulted in the need for a second heating device for the upper section, and ultimately higher production and retail costs. Nevertheless, the appliance found numerous buyers, partly because it saved on space but also because it was beautifully designed. The KF 20 came in a large number of colours, described by Rams as a 'bouquet of flowers on the breakfast table'. Its successor, the KF 21 of 1976, designed by Hartwig Kahlcke, had a downward-pointing handle that was open at the bottom and an adjustable warming plate.

Also in the series: KF 21 (1976)

Plastic, glass, metal
DM 139
Pictured: opposite

Prototypes for a cosmetics set, 1972
Dieter Rams
Braun

6.2–11.5 x 4–5.5 cm in diameter
(2½–4½ x 1½–2¼ in)
0.10–0.21 kg (¼–½ lb)

Plastic
Not released for sale

Here we see Rams's proposal for a set of containers for men's pre-shave and after-shave lotions. The slender, cylindrical form, blue-grey colour and unadorned lettering were intended to distinguish the vessels from more extravagant perfume bottle designs, and to make them appealing to the male consumer.

intercontinental, 1972
Electric shaver
Robert Oberheim, Florian Seiffert,
Dieter Rams

Braun
Shaver: 9.7 × 6.5 × 2.5 cm (3¾ × 2½ ×
1 in); with charging stand: 12.7 × 10.5 ×
2.9 cm (5 × 4 × 1 in)

Shaver: 0.18 kg (½ lb); charging stand:
0.10 kg (¼ lb)
Plastic, metal
DM 172

Following its release in 1972, this
shaver attracted attention for both its
shape and its name, given to it by the
Braun marketing department. At the
time, the term 'intercontinental' was
only used in regard to air travel – now
a shaver could also symbolize the jet-
setting lifestyle. The battery-operated,
cordless shaver was packaged in
stainless steel and black plastic
and a round, grooved power button,
transferred from Florian Seiffert's
cassett shaver (p. 177), was placed
on the front; this reuse of elements
across Braun products made them
instantly recognizable. The compact
and technically advanced design was
intended to appeal to well-travelled
company executives.

phase 3, 1972
Alarm clock
Dieter Rams, Dietrich Lubs
Braun

9.5 × 11 × 6 cm (3¾ × 4¼ × 2½ in)
0.25 kg (½ lb)

Plastic, acrylic
DM 48

Following the release of the phase 1 alarm clock (p. 179), and its successor, the phase 2, Braun transitioned relatively quickly from segmented roller and split-flap displays to analogue designs with traditional clock hands. This approach was first seen in the phase 3 in 1972. The change in mechanics allowed the casing to be more compact, and the use of hands resulted in a more precise measure of time. The device was illuminated from below by a distinct protruding 'nose' positioned beneath the dial. The phase 3's narrow box shape became the standard for all future Braun alarm clocks.

720 / 721, 1972
Dining table with extension leaf
Dieter Rams
Vitsœ

Vitsœ's first table made entirely of
plastic was the 720, a small dining
or breakfast model. In addition,
the company created an extendable
option, the 721, which had a sophisticated mechanism that allowed an
extension leaf to be inserted into the
middle and the table to be substantially
enlarged. The table feet were height-
adjustable, making them suitable
for uneven floors; the legs could also
be removed for easy storage.

720: 71 × 120 × 110 cm (28 × 47¼ ×
43¼ in); 721: 71 × 195 × 110 cm
(28 × 76¾ × 43¼ in)
approx. 40 kg (88¼ lb)

Polystyrene foam, PVC
DM 2,290–2,410 (prices from 1982)

Prototype for a Super-8 pocket movie
camera, 1972
Robert Oberheim
Braun

8 × 16.7 × 4.5 cm (3 × 6½ × 1¾ in)
0.35 kg (¾ lb)

Plastic
Not released for sale

This prototype for a pocket movie
camera takes its basic form from that
of the Super-8 film cartridge. The white
body was combined with a black lens
flap and surrounding; the flap doubled
as a lens cap to protect the glass
during transport. The simple, intuitive
design allowed for the recording of
everyday situations with relatively little
technical understanding.

CSQ 1020, 1973
Quadrophonic preamplifier with SQ
decoder
Dieter Rams

Braun
11 × 40 × 31.5 cm (4¼ × 15¾ × 12½ in)
11 kg (24¼ lb)

Sheet steel, aluminium, plastic
DM 1,560

In the 1970s, audio manufacturers began experimenting with a new approach to sound reproduction using four channels – and four separate speakers – to output from both the front and rear of a hi-fi system. Quadrophonic sound, as it became known, was one of the earliest examples of domestic surround sound technology. Japanese company JVC was an early leader in the field, and Braun also briefly entered the market. However, the company was not entirely convinced of its feasibility and ultimately the venture ended in commercial failure. Rams recalled that it was the conductor Herbert von Karajan – a patient of Werner Kuprian, head of Braun's private

health service – who put a definitive end to the experiment. During one trip to the Braun headquarters, the four-way sound system was demonstrated to him with a request for his opinion. Von Karajan's reply was brief and succinct: his Rolls-Royce stereo was far better.

To make use of the complex new technology, each audio separate required a redesign. Rams's CSQ 1020 preamplifier, produced in a small run of 3,200 units, was equipped with numerous push buttons and sliders and packaged in a regie enclosure. The matching record player, the PSQ 500, a successor to 1968's PS 500 (p. 152), was less demanding and only

required a new pickup, which could be switched out when not in use. After quadrophonic sound failed to take off, Braun's audio engineers embarked on an even more daring foray: their holophonic sound system, featuring nine loudspeakers and two woofers, was presented at the 1979 Internationale Funkausstellung (International Radio Exhibition) in Berlin, and was intended to provide a completely new listening experience. However, Gillette product managers in Boston soon lost interest in the costly pursuit. With a retail price of around 7,000 deutschmarks, the project was considered a bad investment.

sixtant 6007, 1973
Electric shaver
Dieter Rams, Richard Fischer
Braun

11 × 6.4 × 3.1 cm (4½ × 2½ × 1¼ in)
0.3 kg (¾ lb)

Metal, plastic
DM 110

More than a decade after its debut in 1962 (p. 102), the sixtant brand was still a key seller for Braun, sparking a succession of new models in the 1970s. Rams's first contribution to the range was the sixtant 6007, which featured a ribbed circular grip on the front that he carried over from the 6006 model designed by Richard Fischer a year earlier. Sitting above this is a prominent green power button that clearly indicates its function; the colour is a reference to the power buttons Rams used on his high-end audio separates, and an indication of quality and precision. Erwin Braun was quick to recognize and promote the benefits of transferring particular elements from top-of-the-range Braun products to the more affordable models, which ultimately led to higher sales.

sixtant 8008, 1973
Electric shaver
Dieter Rams, Florian Seiffert, Robert Oberheim

Braun
11.2 × 5.8 × 2.8 cm (4½ × 2¼ × 1 in)
0.27 kg (½ lb)

Metal, plastic
DM 102

As chief designer at Braun, Rams was always involved in the design development of new product lines. In 1973, his next big project was the sixtant 8008, which was emerging as Braun's new star model. The front and back are lined in fine horizontal striations and the central switch uses easy-to-read symbols to indicate the off, shave and hair trimmer functions. Unusually for Braun's shaving range, the 8008 was also offered in a brown version. The device features a newly flattened version of the 'Braun compact' foil and cutter cassette, a patented design, which allowed for a flat-topped case. The 8008 was extraordinarily successful in economic terms, with more than 10 million units manufactured – no other shaver had been produced in such large numbers before. The sixtant 5005, a model with a similar design in white, was released in 1984.

Also in the series: sixtant 5005 (1984)

L 308, 1973
Loudspeaker
Dieter Rams
Braun

14.1 × 34.5 × 10.1 cm (5½ × 13½ × 4 in)
6.5 kg (14¼ lb)

Polystyrene
DM 300

This compact loudspeaker with a
plastic enclosure was designed to
accompany the audio 308 compact
system (opposite). The large holes
in the speaker grille are a design
modification from the previous year's
L 260 (p. 186), as is the Braun logo,
which can be rotated depending on
the speaker's orientation.

audio 308, 1973
Compact system
Dieter Rams
Braun

16.7 × 79.7 × 35 cm (6½ × 31½ × 13¾ in)
19 kg (42 lb)

Polystyrene, metal, plastic, acrylic
DM 1,650

'Plastic fantastic' was the catchphrase of the early 1970s, and practically no other material held such predominance in the consumer market. Braun responded to the craze with a whole new generation of audio products that embraced the decade's Pop aesthetic and the lower price point afforded by this novel material. The audio 308 combined radio and record player was tilted at an eight-degree angle towards the user, a feature that was largely determined by the mains transformer being housed in the rear. However, it also pointed towards a more user-friendly operation. The acrylic dust cover was left partially open at the front, allowing access to the most important controls even when closed;

sliders were chosen in reference to professional mixing consoles. Another distinct element is the tapered plinth, which allowed the device to be easily removed after injection moulding. A second version of the design, the audio 308 S, consisted of an aluminium-coloured upper surface, and a black record player and tonearm.

To accompany the sound system, Rams designed matching loud-speakers (opposite) that could be positioned upright or horizontally, or even mounted on a wall. A television set was also planned as part of the series, but did not make it to production (p. 212). The audio 308 was Braun's most successful hi-fi

sound system, with 55,000 units produced across two models. It also influenced other hi-fi devices of the time: the American-German industrial designer Hartmut Esslinger drew on the tilted shape for his Wega Concept 51k system from 1978.

Also in the series: 308 S (1975)

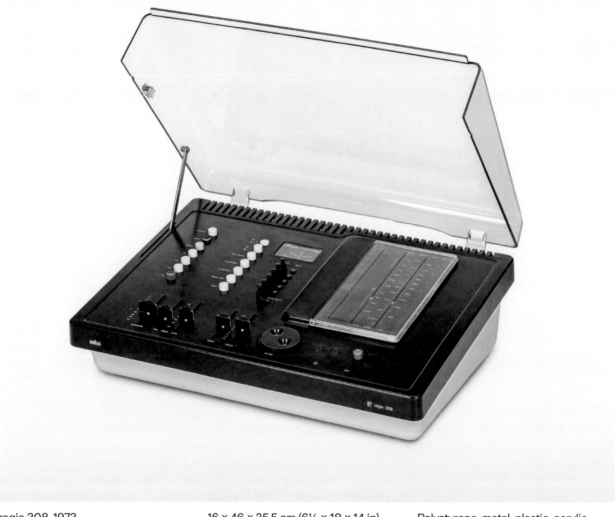

regie 308, 1973
Receiver
Dieter Rams
Braun

16 × 46 × 35.5 cm (6¼ × 18 × 14 in)
10 kg (22 lb)

Polystyrene, metal, plastic, acrylic
DM 1,100

This receiver was uncoupled from the audio 308 compact system (p. 201) to allow its use as an individual module.

Also in the series: regie 308 S (1973), regie 308 F (1974)

PS 358, 1973
Record player
Dieter Rams
Braun

16 × 46 × 35.5 cm (6¼ × 18 × 14 in)
8.4 kg (18½ lb)

Polystyrene, metal, plastic, acrylic
DM 459

This record player was also extracted from the audio 308 compact system (p. 201) and sold as a separate component. It featured a very elegant tonearm with a flat headshell and a striking yellow, teardrop-shaped rotary switch. A total of 7,300 units were produced.

Also in the series: PS 348 (1973)

PS 350, 1973
Record player
Dieter Rams
Braun

17 × 50 × 32 cm (6¾ × 19¾ × 12½ in)
8.5 kg (18¾ lb)

Laminated wood, plastic, sheet steel,
acrylic
DM 498–530

In a further reduction of the PS 358
record player (p. 203), the 350 model
was repackaged in a box-like plinth
with transparent acrylic dust cover –
an addition that Rams was not involved
in designing as he considered it to
be unattractive. Here the intention
was to create a better aesthetic fit with
Braun's wider hi-fi range. The model
was relatively inexpensive and sold
more than 130,000 units.

Also in the series: PS 450 (1973)

audio 400, 1973
Compact system
Dieter Rams
Braun

17 × 75 × 36 cm (6¾ × 29½ × 14 in)
19 kg (42 lb)

Laminated wood, sheet steel, plastic,
acrylic
DM 2,100

As an alternative to the audio 308's
distinctive tilted design (p. 201),
this sound system came in a more
conventional box shape in order to
appeal to the wider, more conservative
market. The 400 had a subtler incline
in its front control panel but retained
the partially open dust cover, allowing
operation when closed. Almost 30,000
units were produced across two models.

Also in the series: audio 400 S (1975)

Nizo spezial 136, 1973
Super-8 movie camera
Robert Oberheim
Braun Nizo

9.7 × 23 × 5.2 cm (3¾ × 9 × 2 in)
0.7 kg (1½ lb)

Aluminium, plastic
DM 698

After Braun released its large-scale
movie camera range, which included
the Nizo S 8 from 1965 (p. 135),
it moved on to a series of smaller
cameras that were cheaper and even
easier to operate. Although it applied
essentially the same design as the
larger models, Braun's intention was
to reach a new target market.

weekend, 1974
Pocket lighter
Dieter Rams, Gugelot Institut, Florian
Seiffert

The weekend lighter was designed
using piezo technology and came
in black or a range of coloured
plastics. Notably, the air intake slots,
which traditionally would have been
horizontal slits, were replaced by
round holes.

Braun
6.9 × 3 × 1.3 cm (2¾ × 1 × ½ in)
0.04 kg (1½ oz)

Plastic, metal
DM 30

energetic (cylindric solar), 1974
Prototype of lighter and storage case
Dieter Rams
Braun

Lighter: 8.8 × 5.3 cm in diameter
(3½ × 2 in); storage case:
12.3 × 7 cm in diameter (4¾ x 2¾ in)
Lighter: 0.23 kg (½ lb);

storage case: 0.08 kg (¼ lb)
Lighter: metal, acrylic glass;
storage case: aluminium, metal foil
Not released for sale

At 600 deutschmarks, the energetic was set to be Braun's most expensive lighter; however, it was only developed to pre-production stage and never made it to the market. Although it retained the shape of Ram's cylindric model (p. 149), the lighter was equipped with a sophisticated photovoltaic energy system, which was still very expensive at the time; the solar cells arranged within the top panel were able to charge the NiCd battery using only normal room lighting. On a single charge, the battery could last for two months with between thirty and forty uses per day. To accompany the lighter, Rams also designed an extravagant aluminium storage case with a bright red interior. Two semi-circular openings are carved into the edge of the lid, creating a feature through which the red plastic backing is visible. Furthermore, the lid could be used upside down as an ashtray, in which case the semi-circular indentations served as a cigarette holder. In conceptual terms, the design represents the successful integration of energy-saving technology into an article of everyday use.

740, 1974
Furniture stacking programme
Dieter Rams
Vitsœ

Stackable disc: 11 × 35 cm in diameter (4¼ × 13¾ in); table tops: 4 × 65/85 cm in diameter (1½ × 25½/33½ in) Stackable disc: 1.5 kg (3¼ lb);

table tops: 3 kg (6½ lb)
Plastic
Stackable disc: DM 39; table tops: DM 229–354 (prices from 1980)

Inspired by his many business trips to Japan and fascination with Japanese culture, Rams designed this modular stacking furniture range for Vitsœ. The individual disc-shaped volumes can be built up by inserting a stabilizing ring in between each layer. Low tables can also be paired with a larger diameter table top. Intended for both indoor and outdoor use, when placed outside, the pieces acquire a dark patina over time, giving them the appearance of stone sculptures.

Prototype for a TV set, 1974
Dieter Rams
Braun

56 × 45 × 32.5 cm (22 × 17¾ × 12¾ in)
8 kg (17½ lb)

Polystyrene, acrylic
Not released for sale

This prototype television set was designed to accompany Rams's 308 audio series (p. 201). Although it wasn't created until 1974, a preliminary draft for a similar design featured in a 1966 article in Braun's staff magazine, the *Braun Betriebsspiegel*. The monitor was separated from the receiver by a rotating stand, enabling it to be turned in different directions. However, as a result of wider economic issues at the time, including the 1973 oil crisis, Braun's sales growth declined considerably in 1974, so the company was cautious about taking on risky new development projects.

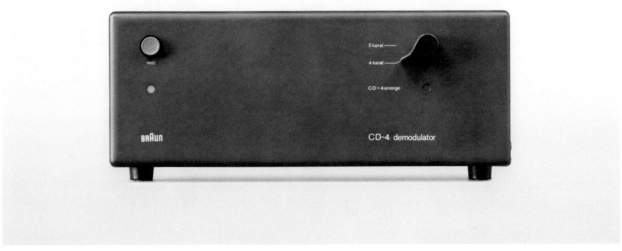

CD-4, 1974
Quadrophonic demodulator
Dieter Rams
Braun

In 1974, a demodulator was added
to the CSQ 1020 quadrophonic
sound system (p. 197). Rams housed
it in an inconspicuous but clearly
structured casing.

11 × 26 × 33.5 cm (4¼ × 10¼ × 13 in)
approx. 5 kg (11 lb)

Sheet steel, aluminium
DM 600

Project Paper Mate, 1974
Writing instruments
Dieter Rams, Dietrich Lubs, Hartwig
Kahlcke, Klaus Zimmermann

Gillette / Paper Mate
Size and weight unknown

Plastic or chromed metal
Not released for sale

A few years after Braun was taken over by Gillette, Rams was invited to its head offices in Boston to discuss opportunities for the design team to work on projects for Gillette's other subsidiaries, one of which was the American writing instrument company Paper Mate. Vincent C Ziegler, chairman and CEO of Gillette at the time, was keen to establish a high-end design vision across the Gillette Group, although sadly Paper Mate did not share his view. Upon presenting the company with designs and sketches for a new product range, Rams recalls the chief executive exclaiming, 'The big boss wants this, but we don't need this.' According to the designer, 'When I delivered the models, they vanished without a trace and were never seen again. I later searched for the prototypes, but couldn't find them.'

Prototypes were created for two Paper Mate ranges, each consisting of a ballpoint pen, fibre-tip pen and mechanical pencil. The models were retractable – with both click-down and turning-mechanism versions included – and came with a removable clip. The design also included a series of cases and sales displays.

Project Paper Mate, 1974
Writing instruments
Dieter Rams, Dietrich Lubs, Hartwig
Kahlcke, Klaus Zimmermann

Gillette / Paper Mate
Size and weight unknown

Plastic, chromed metal, aluminium or
stainless steel
Not released for sale

This alternative Paper Mate model
features a sophisticated turning
mechanism, which doubles as a pen
grip. This striated middle section is
an integral design feature as it allows
the shaft and tip to merge into one
seamless piece. The retractable
function removes the need for a pen
lid, thus providing another opportunity
to enhance the design of the nib. The
close-fitting clip can be opened out
when pressed at the top.

Prototype for a drinking cup, 1975
Dieter Rams
Braun

Cup: 7.2 × 5.6/8 cm in diameter
(2¾ × 2¼/3 in); saucer: 1 × 10.2 cm
in diameter (½ × 4 in)
0.11 kg (¼ lb)

Plastic
Not released for sale

These drinking cups were created
to complement Braun's line of coffee
makers, and marked a first step
towards finding an alternative to
disposable cups used in the office.
The design consists of a reusable
saucer and holder into which a waxed
paper cup can be inserted, resulting
in a sturdy drinking vessel with a
handle. These unrealized prototypes
would serve as inspiration eight years
later for Braun's submission to the
Lufthansa in-flight tableware design
competition (pp. 294–5).

Prototype for a drinking cup, 1975
Dieter Rams
Braun

8 × 6/9 cm in diameter (3 × 2½/3½ in)
0.3 kg (¾ lb)

Plastic
Not released for sale

This second prototype took the
environmental initiative a step further;
here, the paper cup is replaced
altogether by a washable acrylic
insert. In a 1972 report, 'The Limits to
Growth', commissioned by the Club
of Rome – a think tank founded in
1968 by a group of politicians,
scientists, economists and business
leaders from around the globe – the
authors called for urgent reflection
on the environment and its resources.
Its publication had a profound effect
on Rams, and since then, the longevity
of products has played a significant
part in his design process.

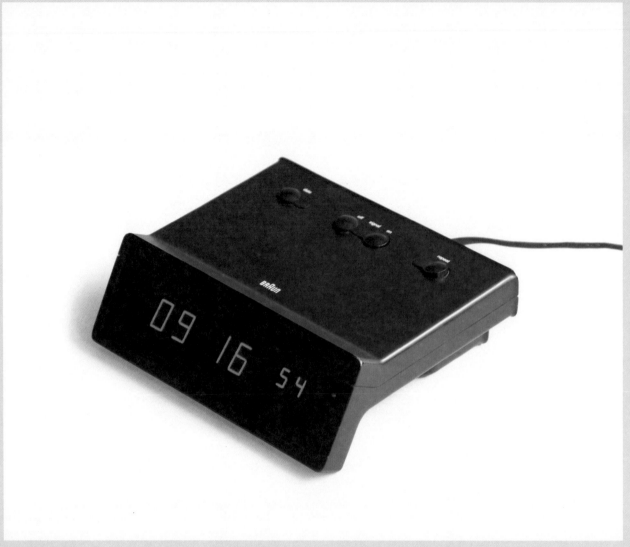

functional, 1975
Alarm clock
Dietrich Lubs
Braun

5.2 × 14.7 × 12.7 cm (2 × 5¾ × 5 in)
0.75 kg (1¾ lb)

Plastic, glass
approx. DM 300

Dietrich Lubs's 'functional' alarm clock houses a large transformer at the rear, while an inclined display occupies the front section. Rocker-style control switches, like those seen on Braun's ABR 21 clock radio from 1978 (pp. 254–5), line the back of the transformer. The sturdy and elegant, fully digital design can be used as an alarm clock or as a desk clock, and, because it operates without mechanical parts, is completely noiseless.

AB 20 (1975)
Alarm clock
Dieter Rams, Dietrich Lubs
Braun

6.9 × 8.6 × 4.8 cm (2¾ × 3½ × 2 in)
0.1 kg (¼ lb)

Plastic, acrylic
DM 48

The precursor to Braun's legendary battery-powered travel alarm clocks – the AB 20 – was created by Rams and Dietrich Lubs in 1975. It was a small, lightweight device that could be used anywhere and was also suitable for travel. Its uncomplicated, intuitive design was accessible for all users, regardless of technical skill; a single, prominent switch on the front turns the alarm on or off. In what was likely an inside joke, the world time zone map, printed on the inside of the cover, does not use Bonn or Berlin to represent Germany, but Frankfurt, home to Braun's headquarters.

The AB 20 drew on past examples for design inspiration – including

Marianne Brandt's table clock from c.1930 and Erich Dieckmann's design from 1931, both of which featured a black dial with contrasting hands and time markings, and Max Bill's 1959 model for Junghans, which was presented in a black box with a centred round dial. However, at that time, Rams and Lubs's approach created a unique selling point within the market. Their perfectly formed timepieces were about more than just craftsmanship and ornamentation; they were about function too.

Similar to the AW 10 wristwatch from 1989 (p. 317), the AB 20 was not sold commercially at first, but was used by Braun as a promotional gift. It soon

became available at specialist retailers and department stores.

Also in the series: color (1975) and tb travel (1981)

TGC 450, 1975
Tape deck
Dieter Rams
Braun

11 × 28.5 × 33.5 cm (4¼ × 11¼ × 13 in)
6 kg (13¼ lb)

Sheet steel, aluminium, plastic, acrylic
DM 898

The TGC 450 tape deck was developed in response to the burgeoning use of compact cassette technology that had been introduced by Philips in the 1960s. Taking advantage of the smaller set-up, Rams designed a top-loading deck and placed the control panel on the front. His intention was to create a resemblance to Braun's regie audio series, from which he also transferred most of the controls. The TGC 450 was produced in a run of 27,000 units.

KH 500, 1975
Stereo headphones
Dieter Rams
Braun

Headband: 20 cm (8 in) in diameter
0.19 kg (½ lb)

Plastic, foam padding
DM 99

To complement Braun's existing range
of closed-back hi-fi headphones,
Rams designed this open-back model
featuring a wide headband. The sides
of the headband are perforated with
large slits in order to cover as little of
the head as possible, resulting in a
more comfortable fit. The pronounced,
leather-covered padding used on the
preceding models was also replaced
by flatter, exposed-foam headphone
cups. A total of 23,000 units of the
headphones were produced.

ET 11 control, 1975
Pocket calculator
Dieter Rams, Dietrich Lubs
Braun / Omron

13.5 × 8.4 × 2.4 cm (5¼ × 3¼ × 1 in)
0.13 kg (¼ lb)

Plastic, acrylic
Price unknown

The ET 11 control calculator was the
result of an initiative from the Braun
sales department, who procured
the design from Japanese electronics
company Omron. The relatively
uninspiring model remained largely
unchanged at first; only the battery
compartment cover, which came in
yellow or orange, was replaced with
a black version featuring the Braun
logo. However, the fact that the device
was externally sourced was reason
enough for the design department to
find a better solution. The result
was the ET 22, which came out the
following year (p. 228).

L 100 compact, 1975
Compact loudspeaker
Dieter Rams
Braun

17.3 × 10.5 × 10.8 cm (6¾ × 4 × 4¼ in)
2.6 kg (¾ lb)

Die-cast aluminium, sheet steel,
aluminium
DM 198

This small two-way speaker with a solid die-cast aluminium enclosure has a surprisingly rich sound. It was intended to be installed on a shelf or as a wall-mounted unit but, above all, it was designed to bring high-quality audio to the car. For this purpose, Rams designed specially padded sides using shock-absorbent material that could be attached when needed, in order to prevent passengers from being injured by the hard metal enclosure. Produced in a run of 55,000 units, the L 100 was issued a patent by the German Patent Office on 8 March 1979.

Also in the series: L 100 auto (1978)

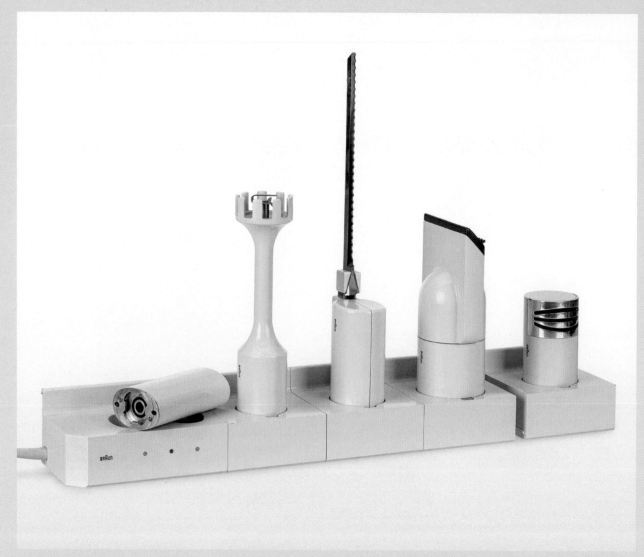

Prototypes for modular kitchen
appliances, 1975
Peter Schneider
Braun

These prototype kitchen appliances
were designed using the modular
concept. Different accessories, such
as an electric knife and a whisk, could
be attached to a cylindrical motor
unit, all of which were stowed in a long,
rectangular base that doubled as a
charging station for the motor.

33.5 × 50 × 8.4 cm (13¼ × 19¾ × 3¼ in)
3.35 kg (7½ lb)

Plastic, metal
Not released for sale

domino set, 1976
Table lighter and ashtrays
Dieter Rams
Braun

As an extension of the T 3 table lighter
from 1970 (p. 170), the modified domino
model was offered as part of a set with
three plastic ashtrays. The ashtrays
have black interiors to keep unsightly
cigarette ash and butts from being too
visible; two semi-circular indentations
in the sides serve as cigarette holders;
and a metal dome in the centre allows
safe extinguishing.

Lighter: 5.5 × 5.5 × 6 cm (2¼ ×
2¼ × 2½ in); ashtrays: 3.4/5.5 ×
7.3 cm in diameter (1¼/2¼ × 3 lb)
Lighter: 0.13 kg (¼ lb);

ashtrays: 0.07/0.09 kg (2½/3¼ oz)
Plastic, metal
DM 78

DN 40 electronic, 1976
Alarm clock
Dieter Rams, Dietrich Lubs
Braun

In addition to roller, split-flap and
analogue clock designs, Braun also
made use of vacuum fluorescent
display (VFD) technology. This
small digital alarm clock, featuring
bright green numbers enclosed
in an extremely pared-back black,
red or white casing, tilts its display
downwards towards the viewer.
With its characteristically intuitive
user interface, the DN 40 is a prime
example of Rams's view that good
design is as little design as possible.

5.3 × 10.7 × 11.2 cm (2 × 4¼ × 4½ in)
0.4 kg (1 lb)

Plastic, acrylic
Price unknown

regie 550, 1976
Receiver
Dieter Rams
Braun

11 × 50 × 33.5 cm (4¼ × 19¾ × 13¼ in)
14 kg (31 lb)

Sheet steel, aluminium, plastic, acrylic
DM 1,760

Produced in a run of 18,500 units, the regie 550 receiver was the highest-performing model in its series, representing the racing car of Braun's hi-fi sound systems. Switching on the power is akin to starting a Porsche 911: the audio announces itself with a deep starting tone; the two wafer-thin pointers of the level meters spring into action; and the lights come alive. When matched with the proper loudspeakers, the sound can reach levels close to those produced by a Porsche engine. With a weight of 14 kg (31 lb) and an all-metal design, even the appearance of the regie devices is robust. The innovative, convex push-button controls could also be found on the ET 22 control pocket calculator (p. 228).

ET 22 control, 1976 / ET 23 control,
1977 (pictured)
Pocket calculator
Dieter Rams, Dietrich Lubs

Braun
14.5 × 8 × 2.3 cm (5¾ × 3 × 1 in)
0.14 kg (¼ lb)

Plastic, acrylic
DM 76

At first glance, it is the small but striking elements that distinguish this design from the original Omron calculator (p. 222); however, on closer inspection, other crucial details reveal themselves. The previously squat form has been elongated and the rounding of the corners reduced, creating a new set of proportions and giving the device a clear orientation. Perhaps more significant was the switch from concave to convex push buttons, which not only improved operating function, but added elegance to the design; this was highlighted by the buttons' polished surface and the subtle colour scheme of black and brown, paired with a contrasting yellow. What remained

unchanged were the basic rectangular shape of the body, the digital display with its green numerals on a black background, and the technology. All Braun calculators, with the exception of the ET 44 (p. 261), were manufactured in Asia.

The ET 22 is an excellent example of Braun's ability to successfully apply tried and tested design elements to a number of different devices: the distinctive push buttons were identical to those used on the regie 550 receiver (p. 227), which was being developed at the same time; the construction of the protective slipcase, which automatically turns the power button to 'off' when the

calculator is stowed, is based on that of the cassett shaver from 1970 (p. 177); and the yellow equals sign reflects the colour used for the second hand of Braun's alarm clocks from 1975 onwards. These morphological transfers contributed significantly to Braun's corporate design image.

L 200, 1976
Bookshelf loudspeaker
Dieter Rams
Braun

25.5 × 16 × 15 cm (10 × 6¼ × 6 in)
4.2 kg (9¼ lb)

Laminated wood, aluminium
DM 198

This three-way loudspeaker was
designed for Braun's slim-line audio
series. It has an outwardly curving
grille made of perforated metal, which
physically projects itself towards the
listener. The L 200 was produced in
an impressive run of 44,500 units.

Prototype for an electric kettle, 1976
Dieter Rams, Jürgen Greubel
Braun

21.5 × 22 × 13.5 cm (8½ × 8¾ × 5¼ in)
0.8 kg (1¾ lb)

Plastic
Not released for sale

This kettle consists of a plastic reservoir and gently angled handle. The triangular shape of the volume, narrow at the front and wider at the back, gives the kettle a distinct orientation, and therefore a clear function. A transparent acrylic window runs the height of the reservoir at the front, allowing the water level to be checked.

Prototype for a single-serve coffee
maker, 1976
Dieter Rams, Jürgen Greubel
Braun

Size and weight unknown

Plastic, metal
Not released for sale

This single-serve coffee maker was
designed to cater to the growing
number of one-person households.
It had capacity for one cup of coffee,
which was brewed in a pot at the top.
The black water reservoir underneath
flares slightly at the base and there is
a single push-button switch. The hot
water is fed into the top section via a
clear external tube to a filter inserted
into the aluminium pot. The result is a
piece of kitchen sculpture that is as
functional as it is striking and beautiful.

Prototype for an iron, 1976
Dieter Rams, Jürgen Greubel
Braun

10.2 × 25 × 12 cm (4 × 9¾ × 4¾ in)
1.25 kg (2¾ lb)

Plastic, metal, acrylic
Not released for sale

This novel design for an iron was
developed under great secrecy in
Rams's workshop at home. The
monolithic body melds the heating
and ironing elements with the handle,
creating an organic shape that
provides the perfect platform for the
curved temperature-setting display.
Numerous versions were developed
but, despite its originality, the design
was never realized.

Cricket, 1976
Pre-production models for
a disposable lighter
Dieter Rams

When Gillette purchased Braun in
1967, its CEO Vincent C Ziegler was
intent on bringing Braun design to
Gillette's other subsidiaries, although
he was not entirely successful.
Rams designed this disposable
Cricket lighter but it was not put into
production. The economical diamond-
shaped cross-section would have
allowed several lighters to be tightly
packed together, therefore saving
on space.

Gillette / Cricket
8.1 × 2.7 × 1.5 cm (3¼ × 1 × ¾ in)
0.01 kg (½ oz)

Plastic, metal
Not released for sale

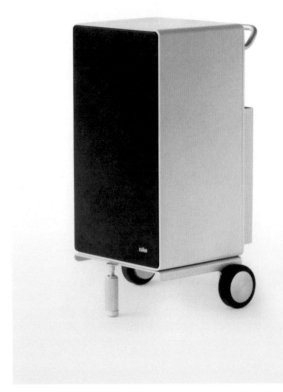
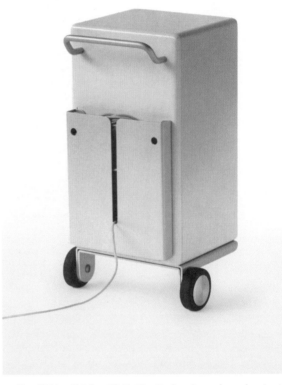

Prototype for a portable hi-fi sound system and loudspeakers, 1976
Dieter Rams
Braun / Vincent C Ziegler

Hi-fi: 15.5 × 54 × 28 cm (6 × 21¼ × 11 in); loudspeakers: unknown
Hi-fi: 3 kg (6½ lb); loudspeakers: unknown

Hi-fi: Plastic; loudspeakers: laminated wood, aluminium, rubber
Not released for sale

Rams designed this portable hi-fi sound system and set of loudspeakers simultaneously, although neither project progressed beyond the early prototype stage. The hi-fi was proposed in a bid to save Braun's steadily declining audio sector, which was beginning to become a financial burden for the company. For its design, Rams drew on the regie sound system models for inspiration but also added a cassette player. The loudspeakers, conversely, were developed at the request of Vincent C Ziegler, former CEO of Gillette, who wanted a device that people could use while having outdoor gatherings and barbecues. Although little information about the project has been retained, it is likely that an existing Braun loudspeaker model was used, for which Rams designed the mobile enclosure.

2056 sound, 1976
Super-8 audio movie camera
Peter Schneider
Braun Nizo

15.7 × 25.8 × 7 cm (6¼ × 10¼ × 2¾ in)
1.65 kg (3½ lb)

Aluminium, sheet steel, plastic
DM 1,898

From 1976, Braun began selling
movie cameras with sound recording
capabilities. The new models kept
the same basic structure and layout
established by Robert Oberheim,
although Peter Schneider was now
the lead designer. Rather than its
usual vertical orientation, the handle
was attached diagonally to the front
of the camera.

PS 550, 1977
Record player
Dieter Rams
Braun

11.5 × 50 × 33.5 cm (4½ × 19¾ × 13¼ in)
7.3 kg (16 lb)

Sheet steel, plastic, acrylic
DM 700

This record player was designed as
part of Braun's slim-line sound system
series, in which all products were
given a height of only 65 mm (2½ in),
not including the dust cover. The
device featured a touch-sensitive
tonearm operator; by placing a finger
in the indentations in the platter,
the tonearm is activated and, when
turning the platter in either direction,
the tonearm follows accordingly. This
feature introduced a novel form of user
interaction with the device. Across
three models, more than 44,000 units
of the record player were produced.

Also in the series: 550 S (1977), P 501
(1981)

P 4000, 1977
Audio system
Dieter Rams
Braun

12 × 87 × 34 cm (4¾ × 34¼ × 13½ in)
25 kg (55 lb)

Sheet steel, plastic, acrylic
DM 1,298

In 1977, the P 4000 audio system
with record player or tape deck
(or both) came onto the market as
the successor to Braun's audio 1
(p. 88) and 2 (p. 121) sound systems.
The individual compact units proved
popular, but the larger, integrated
versions were not economically
successful. Across the three models,
a total of 13,500 units were produced.

Rams paired the classic box construction with an elegantly sloping
front panel that featured an array
of buttons, tuning scales and
slide controls.

Also in the series: PC 4000 and
C 4000 (1977)

PDS 550, 1977
Record player
Dieter Rams
Braun

11 × 50 × 33 cm (4¼ × 19¾ × 13 in)
7 kg (15½ lb)

Sheet steel, plastic, acrylic
DM 998

The successor to Braun's PS 550
record player (p. 237) no longer
required its user to physically activate
the controls. The control buttons and
electronic tonearm lifter were replaced
by sensors, which operated the device
automatically. Only the power switch
remained a physical push button.
The PDS 550 was produced in a run
of 30,000 units.

Also in the series: P 701 (1981)

DW 20, 1977
Digital wristwatch
Dieter Rams, Dietrich Lubs
Braun

0.7 x 3.5 cm in diameter (¼ x 1½ in)
0.07 kg (2½ oz)

Duralumin and chrome plating or
titanium oxide, stainless steel
DM 342

Braun's first design for a digital watch
adopts the round face of an analogue
model, but pairs this with a vacuum
fluorescent display (VFD) in a narrow,
framed screen in the centre. It
demonstrates the designers' attempt
to establish a new form, but it is not
entirely convincing. The DW 30 watch
(p. 252) from the following year was
more successful in this respect.

ET 33 control LCD, 1977
Pocket calculator with case
Dieter Rams, Dietrich Lubs
Braun

13.6 × 7.6 × 1.3 cm (5½ × 3 x ½ in)
0.08 kg (2¾ oz)

Plastic, acrylic
DM 76

The ET 33 came onto the market in
1977. Compared to its predecessor,
the ET 22 (p. 228), it is much flatter at
13 mm (½ in) and has a liquid crystal
display (LCD) with black digits on a
light background. The protective case
was also altered, and now came in the
form of a hard plastic shell, which was
attached to the device and doubled
as a holder when in use. The push
buttons for the memory functions were
changed from brown to dark green.

L 1030, 1977
Floor-standing speaker
Dieter Rams
Braun

70 x 31 x 26 cm (27½ x 12¼ x 10¼ in)
18 kg (39¾ lb)

Wood, aluminium
DM 798

This floor-standing loudspeaker first came on sale in 1977. The perforated speaker grille is raised above a plinth, elevating the design both physically and aesthetically; two prominent rotary switches positioned on the top control the mid- and high-frequency sound ranges. Produced in an initial run of 17,200 units, the L 1030 sparked a number of different iterations: the GSL 1030 and L 1030-8 (of 1978 and 1979) use the same form as the L 1030 but do not have level controls; simultaneously a series of three-way studio monitors (SM 1002 to SM 1005) was developed as part of the integral studio system (p. 248), which have the same grilles as the original model but no plinth, so could be placed on either

a bookshelf or the floor. The SM 1006 and SM 1006 TC models followed, but were once again placed on plinths. All the different model versions made for a rather confusing product family.

Also in the series: L 1030-4 US (1977), GSL 1030 (1978), L 1030-8 (1979); SM 1002, SM 1003, SM 1004 and SM 1005 (1978), SM 1006 TC (1979), SM 1006 and SM 1001 (1980)

LW 1, 1978
Subwoofer, coffee-table speaker
Dieter Rams, Peter Hartwein
Braun

37 × 70 × 70 cm (14½ × 27½ × 27½ in)
33 kg (72¾ lb)

Wood, aluminium
DM 798

This subwoofer brought even more
intense bass sounds into the living
room, most certainly designed in
response to the proliferation of high-
octane pop and rock music being
released at the time by artists such as
Led Zeppelin, Pink Floyd, David Bowie
and Michael Jackson – although even
Beethoven sounded better on this
loudspeaker. Produced in a small run
of 1,600 units, the dual-function device
could also be used as a side table.

Jafra, 1978
Cosmetics containers
Dieter Rams, Peter Schneider
Gillette / Jafra

Various sizes and weights

Plastic
Not released for sale

In collaboration with Peter Schneider, Rams designed numerous product bottles, jars and tubes for the Gillette cosmetics subsidiary, Jafra. In addition, he was commissioned to redesign the entrance and foyer areas of the company's Malibu offices, as well as a decorative fountain outside, which he completed in partnership with Olson Architects of Santa Barbara. Jafra was founded in 1956 by husband-and-wife team Jan and Frank Day as a direct-to-consumer company supported by a team of independent consultants. The name Jafra is a combination of the founders' first names, Ja(n) and Fra(nk).

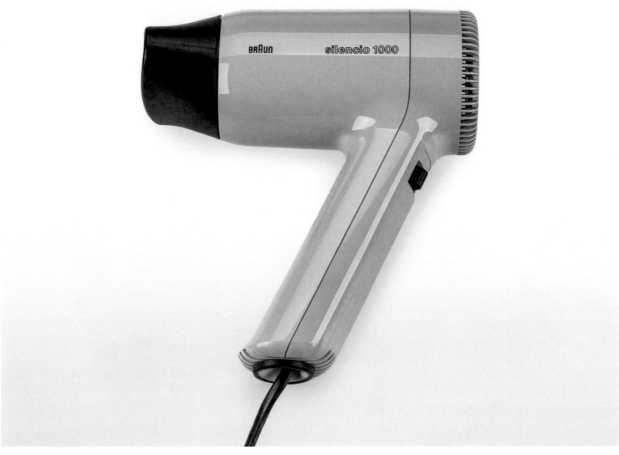

PGC 1000, 1978 / P 1000, 1988
(pictured)
Hair dryer
Dieter Rams, Robert Oberheim,

Jürgen Greubel
Braun
16 × 15 × 7 cm (6¼ × 6 × 2¾ in)
0.25 kg (½ lb)

Plastic
DM 29

The handle position on this hair dryer caused a heated discussion between Braun's sales and design departments. The sales team, which at the time still referred to itself the 'business department', had commissioned the Technische Universität Darmstadt to carry out a study on the ergonomically correct position of a hair dryer handle, and the resulting research found that it should be angled backwards. While this may have been suitable for use by hairdressers, the design team argued that a forward-angled handle made more sense for drying one's own hair. Ultimately, Braun's designers won the dispute and, with the support of CEO Paul Stern, were able to implement their proposal.

Also in the series: P/PE 1500 (1981), PGS 1000 and PGS/PGC/PGA/PGD/ PGM/PGI/PS 1200 (1982), P/PE 1600 (1985), PX 1200 and P 1100 (1988), PX 1600 and PXE 1600 (1993)

T 301, 1978 / TS 501, 1978 (pictured)
Tuner
Dieter Rams, Peter Hartwein
Braun

6.5 × 50 × 34.8 cm (2½ × 19¾ × 13¾ in)
5 kg (11 lb)

Sheet steel, die-cast aluminium
DM 698

Following on from Braun's modular hi-fi systems of the late 1950s and 1960s – such as studio 2 (p. 53), the high-end 1000 series (pp. 130–1) and its compact regie devices (p. 153) – Rams embarked on a new, larger range of hi-fi separates in the late 1970s. The extremely low height of only 6.5 cm (2½ in) is a particularly striking feature that required a new type of flat transformer; as none were available on the market, Braun engineers were forced to develop their own. A series of red and green LEDs line the width of the tuner, and as the frequency increases, so do the number of activated lights. The more powerful TS 501 model (pictured) has an additional automatic tuning function, and a rocker switch instead of a rotary switch. Across the two tuners, Braun produced 20,500 units.

A 301, 1978 / A 501, 1978 (pictured)
Amplifier
Dieter Rams, Peter Hartwein
Braun

6.5 × 50 × 34.8 cm (2½ × 19¾ x 13¾ in)
8 kg (17½ lb)

Sheet steel, die-cast aluminium
DM 698

As with the other devices in the 301/501 series, the extremely low-slung design of the A 301 amplifier required new transformer technology and a compact arrangement for the electronics. The impressive device, together with its more powerful counterpart, the A 501 (pictured), was considered the gold standard in Braun amplifiers at the time. However, both models would soon be surpassed by the AP 701 power amplifier, which was identical in appearance but had improved performance. Across the three amplifier iterations, almost 19,000 units were produced.

Although the devices appear at first glance to be highly technical, as suggested by the the detailed typography on a black or grey enclosure, once in use they display a more playful and lively nature. The two centrally located LED strips are particularly eye-catching as they flicker to life to track the level of output transmitted to the loudspeakers. The casing is contructed from a continuous sheet of folded metal secured at the front with two black Allen screws. Striking die-cast metal heat sinks lining either side of the device hint at its high-powered capabilities. Despite the amplifier's understated design, with its monochromatic housing and subtle hints of colour in the push-button switches and LEDs, it presents a powerful image when in operation.

Also in the series: AP 701 (1980)

RA 1 analog, 1978 / RS 1 synthesizer,
1978 (pictured)
Analogue receiver and synthesizer
Dieter Rams, Peter Hartwein

Braun
6.5 × 60.5 × 34.8 cm (2½ × 23¾ × 13¾ in)
9 kg (19¾ lb)

Sheet steel, die-cast aluminium
DM 1,198

As an alternative to the T 301 tuner
and A 301 amplifier (pp. 246–7), the
two components were combined into
a single device that was available
in either analogue or digital formats.
Producing 14,200 units across the two
models, Braun named its new offering
the integral studio system, which was
designed to be even flatter and more
compact than competing Japanese
devices. Rams placed the amplifier on
the left and the receiver on the right,
and designed the width of the casing
to match that of the PC 1 combined
cassette recorder and record player
(opposite), which allowed it to be
integrated with other modular devices.
All devices in the integral studio
system have a solid sheet steel and

die-cast aluminium chassis, and
together represent a culmination of
hi-tech and high-design aesthetics,
making them suitable for any
professional or domestic setting.
This was the last of Braun's sound
systems to be manufactured in
Germany; thereafter production
would move to the Far East.

PC 1, 1978
Combined cassette recorder and
record player
Dieter Rams, Peter Hartwein

Braun
11 × 60.5 × 33.5 cm (4¼ × 23¾ × 13¼ in)
15 kg (33 lb)

Sheet steel, acrylic, plastic, rubber
DM 1,998

The PC 1 combined cassette recorder
and record player was designed
to match the RA 1 analog and RS 1
synthesizer (opposite). It incorporated
the PDS 550 record player (p. 239),
which had been released a year
earlier as a standalone unit, but the
system also featured a cassette
recorder capable of high-quality
synchronization. The dust cover is
made of tinted acrylic, similar to
those used on Braun's 'Snow White's
Coffin' SK designs. A total of 9,300
units of the PC 1 were produced.

Also in the series: PC 1 A (1979)

regie 550 d, 1978
Digital receiver
Dieter Rams
Braun

11 × 50 × 33.5 cm (4¼ × 19¾ × 13¼ in)
14 kg (31 lb)

Sheet steel, aluminium, plastic, acrylic
DM 1,498

The top model in the regie series
(p. 227) was later released with a digital
transmitter frequency display, although
the original analogue pointers were
retained as a marker of precision. This
was not the case with the previous
year's regie 530, which only used a
digital display. The regie 550 d was
produced in a small run of 2,400 units.

AB 21 s, 1978
Alarm clock
Dietrich Lubs, Dieter Rams
Braun

This compact alarm clock features
a large stop button running the upper
width of the device, making it easy
to hit when half-asleep. The lettering
on either side of the dial adds to the
overall composition of the device,
creating a more balanced design.

Also in the series: AB 22 (1982)

7.5 × 8.2 × 4.2 cm (3 × 3¼ × 1¾ in)
0.1 kg (¼ lb)

Plastic
DM 39

DW 30, 1978
Quartz wristwatch
Dieter Rams, Dietrich Lubs
Braun

4 × 2.8 × 0.7 cm (1½ x 1 × ¼ in)
0.03 kg (1 oz)

Metal, chrome plating, glass, leather
DM 445

Unlike the DW 20 of 1977 (p. 240), the DW 30 presents a more convincing package for a digital watch. The rectangular display screen is positioned in a square frame, which extends seamlessly into a black strap. Here, the full effect of Braun's signature black-and-silver colour combination can be appreciated. A slightly raised panel separates the top section of watch face, which houses the technology and features a small Braun logo. Below the display screen are two adjustment buttons in the shape of elongated semicircles.

travel 1000, 1978
Prototype for a miniature world-band
receiver
Dieter Rams

Braun
9 × 24 × 4 cm (3½ × 9½ × 1½ in)
0.5 kg (1 lb)

Plastic
Not released for sale

Rams and his design team submitted
a proposal for a miniature receiver in
an attempt to keep Braun's audio arm
in operation, basing their work on
Braun's pocket radio models from
the 1950s; however, it was not well
received by the company's management. The oblong-shaped device has
the display on the left, while the right
side is rounded to house a circular
loudspeaker. The control buttons are
positioned in between.

ABR 21 signal radio, 1978 / ABR 21 FM,
1978 (pictured)
Clock radio
Dieter Rams, Dietrich Lubs
Braun

11.5 × 18 × 6.7 cm (4½ × 7 × 2½ in)
0.5 kg (1 lb)

Plastic
DM 129

It is one thing to hear a clock alarm,
whatever the tone, going off in the
morning, but it is quite another to
wake up to the sound of your favourite
radio station. Following Braun's early
entry into the electric alarm clock
business with the phase 1 in 1971
(p. 179), it seemed a natural progression
for the company to integrate its core
speciality, radio. For their debut in the
field, Rams and Dietrich Lubs took the
opportunity to showcase the rocker
switch developed in 1975 for the
functional digital alarm clock (p. 218),
which comprised two connected
circles, and placed four switches
along the top edge to control all the
necessary functions. The concentric
shaping of this rocker switch is
reflected in the two circles formed
by the clock face and the tuning scale
surrounding the speaker grille on the
front. This side-by-side arrangement
of clock and tuner could be seen
much earlier in the D-25 clock radio
by Crosley Radio Corp., from c.1951.
However, the popular North American
design took its inspiration from the
flamboyant Streamline Moderne style;
the ABR 21's Minimalist, angular design
was available in a simple black or white.

outdoor 2000, 1978
Prototype for a portable sound system
Dieter Rams
Braun

28 × 47 × 17 cm (11 × 18½ × 6¾ in)
8 kg (17½ lb)

Plastic, metal, aluminium
Not released for sale

In 1978, Rams designed a portable audio player for use outdoors. Arranged across two interconnecting, angular volumes, the hi-fi was slid open for use, revealing a black control panel and upright cassette player. The powerful device was designed in the tradition of the T 1000 (p. 106) and T 2002 (p. 167) receivers. What is remarkable is its trapezoidal construction with integrated loud-speakers; good sound was more important than good radio reception at parties. The device was intended to be a high-quality alternative to the powerful ghetto blasters that were popular at the time. Although it never went into production, Braun applied for a patent on 3 March 1979.

C 301, 1978 / C 301 M, 1979 (pictured)
Cassette deck
Dieter Rams, Peter Hartwein
Braun

11 × 50 × 34.5 cm (4¼ × 19¾ × 13½ in)
8 kg (17½ lb)

Sheet steel, plastic
DM 798

This cassette deck was designed as an addition to the regie audio series. The control buttons are based on those of the regie 550 (p. 227), and two strips of LEDs indicate the input signals. The cassette is positioned upright on the front panel; its orientation bears a resemblance to larger reel-to-reel tape recorders. Across two models, 48,000 units of the C 301 were produced.

audio additiv, 1978
Study for a hi-fi sound system
Dieter Rams, Roland Ullmann
Braun

Various sizes and weights

Plastic, acrylic, wood
Not released for sale

These scale models for a novel sound
system suffered the same fate as
Rams's outdoor 2000 portable device
(p. 256) and travel 1000 pocket radio
(p. 253); Braun's American owners
were no longer prepared to continue
in the loss-making audio sector. Had
the highly geometric, entirely new-
look modular design language come
to fruition, it would have set itself apart
from the designs of Braun's past.
The name 'additiv' was derived from
the active speakers intended for the
system, to which accessories
for boosting power levels could
be added.

LC 3 in concert, 1978
Shelf or wall-mounted loudspeakers
Dieter Rams, Peter Hartwein
Braun

44 × 28 × 23 cm (17¼ × 11 × 9 in)
7.5 kg (16½ lb)

Laminated wood or walnut veneer,
fabric
DM 248

In 1978, Braun released these inexpensive 'in concert' series loud-speakers, and went on to sell 50,000 units. However, the acoustic quality did not compare to that of Braun's earlier hi-fi speakers. In order to keep production costs as low as possible, the designers chose a rectangular design and used a fabric cover; the strip at the base was left uncovered. The cheapest model, the ic 50, cost only 149 deutschmarks.

Also in the series: ic 50, ic 70 and ic 90 (1979)

ET 44 control CD, 1978
Pocket calculator
Dietrich Lubs
Braun

14 × 7.3 cm × 1.2 cm (5½ × 3 × ½ in)
0.07 kg (2½ oz)

Plastic, acrylic
DM 62

Similar to its predecessors, the ET 22
and ET 23 (p. 228), Dietrich Lubs's
ET 44 pocket calculator features
elongated memory-function buttons;
all of Braun's later models only used
round buttons. In a possible attempt
to lessen its dependence on Asian
construction and manufacturing
technology, the ET 44 was the only
pocket calculator to be designed
entirely by Braun engineers and
manufactured in the company's
Marktheidenfeld factory, in Bavaria.

SM 2150, 1979
Floor-standing studio monitor
Dieter Rams, Peter Hartwein,
Peter Schneider

Braun
148.5 × 29 × 29 cm
(58½ × 11½ × 11½ in)
46 kg (101½ lb)

Lacquered wood, aluminium, metal
DM 1,798

Produced in a small run of 800 units,
this two-component tower monitor
signified the end of Braun's expensive
loudspeaker technology. However, it
was not lost altogether; Braun's sound
engineers later founded their own
company, Canton, in the Taunus region
of Germany, where they continued
to develop ideas that had first formed
at Braun.

DN 50, 1979
Alarm clock
Ludwig Littmann
Braun

7.5 × 11.1 × 15 cm (3 × 4½ × 6 in)
0.35 kg (¾ lb)

Plastic
DM 82

This small digital alarm clock takes
its right-angled shape from its two
component parts – the display and the
stand – a construction that means only
the clock face is visible from the front.

sixtant 4004, 1979
Electric shaver
Dieter Rams, Robert Oberheim,
Roland Ullmann

Braun
12 × 6 × 2.5 cm (4¾ × 2½ × 1 in)
0.3 kg (¾ lb)

Metal, plastic
DM 84

Although Braun's micron shaver range
had arrived on the market in 1976,
its sixtant models in several different
versions were offered as cheaper
alternatives until 1991. The shape
of this shaver resembles that of the
sixtant 8008 from 1973 (p. 199).

Also in the series: compact S (1979)

micron plus, 1979 / micron plus de luxe, 1980 (pictured)
Rechargeable electric shaver
Roland Ullmann

Braun
11.5 × 6 × 3.2 cm (4½ × 2½ × 1¼ in)
0.3 kg (¾ lb)

Plastic, aluminium, stainless steel
DM 149

Braun's micron shaver range, which began with the original 'micron' model in 1976, unveiled a novel design element that many product designers still use today: a tactile grip that combined both hard and soft plastics to create a comfortable, non-slip surface that had a completely different feel. This unusual quality was the result of an innovative injection moulding technique that Braun's engineers developed in collaboration with plastic manufacturer Bayer, which allowed both hard and soft states to be produced in a single process. In a later iteration of the design, the micron plus deluxe of 1980 (pictured), Bayer and Braun advanced the technology further to combine a soft plastic grip

with a hard aluminium case, resulting in a new generation of high-quality shavers. All micron plus models were cordless and came with a rechargeable battery unit.

Also in the series: micron 2000 (1979)

Nizo integral 7, 1979
Super-8 audio movie camera
Peter Schneider
Braun Nizo

17.5 × 28 × 7 cm (7 × 11 × 2¾ in)
1.25 kg (2¾ lb)

Plastic
DM 1,098

The 'integral' movie camera range
debuted a new design for the Braun–
Nizo collaboration. Peter Schneider
retained the diagonal handle position
of the preceding 2056 sound model
(p. 236), but integrated a microphone
on a telescopic rod. The angled
positioning allowed the microphone
to be as far away as possible from the
noise of the camera motor, while still
benefiting from the convenience of
a built-in audio device. The camera
also featured a new arrangement of
controls, which swapped the previous
rotary designs for a series of slide
switches, making adjustments
much quicker.

SM 1002 S, 1979
Shelf or wall-mounted studio monitor
Dieter Rams, Peter Schneider
Braun

30.5 × 30.5 × 17.5 cm (12 × 12 × 7 in)
5 kg (11 lb)

Laminated wood, anodized aluminium
DM 298

This powerful rectangular studio
monitor is ideal for mounting on a shelf.
The rounded corners of the speaker
grille have a larger radius than those
of the surrounding enclosure, resulting
in a subtle spandrel in each corner
that visually emphasizes the three-
dimensional form of the grille.

1980–1989

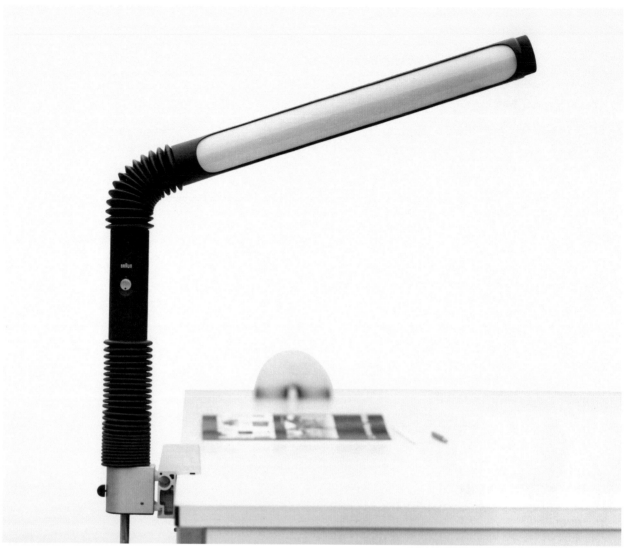

RS 20, 1980
Prototype for a desk lamp
Dieter Rams
Braun

Size and weight unknown

Metal, plastic
Not released for sale

Rams put forward a proposal for a
desk-mounted lamp in 1980, although
it was never realized. A joint made of
flexible tubing connecting the vertical
and horizontal arms of the lamp allows
the position of the light to be adjusted.

RS 10, 1980
Prototype for a desk lamp
Dieter Rams
Braun

Size and weight unknown

Metal, plastic
Not released for sale

In addition to the RS 20 prototype
(opposite), Rams proposed a second
Braun lamp, but this was also a non-
starter. The horizontal lamp holder
could be folded down over the vertical
support arm when not in use, which
led the sales department to consider
offering it as a travel lamp.

H 80, 1980
Prototype for a fan heater
Dieter Rams
Braun Española

24.7 × 12 × 18.5 cm (9¾ × 4¾ × 7¼ in)
1.15 kg (2½ lb)

Plastic
Not released for sale

This combined heater and cooling fan was developed together with Braun Española and was intended for the Spanish market. Due to mild winters, many houses in southern Spain do not have heating, while the summers can be very warm; the H 80 was designed for both purposes, and was intended to fill a gap in the market before the introduction of air conditioning systems. The top section of the upright box is chamfered, providing a surface for two large rotary switches that control the temperature and fan speed. Air is sucked through the side and blown out from the front through large horizontal slots. At the top of the back of the prototype there is a recessed handle for transport; a wall-mounting bracket for stationary use was also devised.

Prototype for a hot air brush, c.1980
Dieter Rams, Jürgen Greubel
Braun

9.5 × 21 × 10.5 cm (3¾ × 8¼ × 4 in)
0.45 kg (1 lb)

Plastic
Not released for sale

This hot air brush was designed as an alternative to a hair dryer, and would have been particularly suitable for long hair. With its handle set at a slight angle, the design reflects that set by the PGC 1000 hair dryer from 1978 (p. 245).

atelier, 1980–90
Hi-fi sound system
Peter Hartwein, Dieter Rams
Braun

69 × 44.5 × 37 cm (27¼ × 17½ × 14½ in)
Various weights

Sheet steel, plastic, aluminium
See individual models for further
specifications

Braun's final addition to the 'atelier' hi-fi series spanned a decade of production and four product generations. The main components comprised a tuner, amplifier, pre-amplifier, receiver, record player, loudspeaker, cassette deck, CD player, pedestal, television and VHS video recorder, as well as a remote control to operate the various devices. The system was initially conceived as an inexpensive alternative to Braun's slim-line range (p. 237), from which it adopted the low-slung height of 6.5 cm (2½ in); the edges of each device are chamfered at the top and bottom, adding to their already thin appearance, and help to visually unify the range. Every component was

manufactured by one of several different companies in the Far East, and with each successive model, the technology became more powerful and consequently more expensive.

In 1981, Gillette sold 80 per cent of its shares in Braun's loss-making hi-fi audio division to Godehard Günther, the German-American founder of a/d/s (Analogue and Digital Systems), who wanted to keep it going under the Braun brand. However, the company had little success, particularly in the United States, and continued to lose money. In 1989, Gillette bought back Günther's shares but just one year later, on 11 June 1990, the managing director of a/d/s, Ernst F Ortmann,

announced the end of Braun's hi-fi production: 'As part of its strategic planning for the company's future business activities, the board of directors of Braun AG has decided to phase out its hi-fi business in the coming 1990–91 season.' The atelier sound systems planned for that season were sold as the Last Edition range, and following a spectacular, 2.5 million-deutschmark advertising campaign by the Saarbrücken-based agency Maksimovic & Partners, 6,900 numbered systems, without boxes, priced at between 5,000 and 10,450 deutschmarks, found buyers within six months.

275

T 1, 1980
Tuner for the atelier system
Peter Hartwein, Dieter Rams
Braun

6.5 × 44.5 × 37 cm (2½ × 17½ × 14½ in)
6 kg (13¼ lb)

Sheet steel, plastic, aluminium
DM 468

The tuner for the atelier system has an
interface that is stripped down to the
essentials: the frequency display is
fully digital; two rows of LEDs indicate
the output level; and the controls that
are seldom used are hidden behind a
flap, leaving only four main operating
buttons, the tuning dial and Braun's
familiar green power switch. Across
two models, 20,000 units of the tuner
were produced.

Also in the series: T 2 (1982)

A 1, 1980 / A 2, 1982 (pictured)
Amplifier for the atelier system
Peter Hartwein, Dieter Rams
Braun

6.5 × 44.5 × 37 cm (2½ × 17½ × 14½ in)
9 kg (19¾ lb)

Sheet steel, plastic, aluminium
DM 598

The atelier amplifiers have a similar construction to that of the tuners (opposite). The lesser-used rotary switches for treble and bass are concealed behind a hinged flap; a large round rotary switch circled by white line markings indicates volume adjustment; two toggle switches control the function settings. A total of 20,000 units of the amplifier were produced.

C 1, 1980
Tape recorder for the atelier system
Peter Hartwein, Dieter Rams
Braun

6.5 × 44.5 × 37 cm (2½ × 17½ × 14½ in)
8.3 kg (18¼ lb)

Sheet steel, plastic
DM 848

The C 1 tape recorder featured a novel front-loading tray compartment in which tapes were played horizontally rather than vertically, with the drawer either pulled out or positioned inside the device – the first occasion that Braun had used such an approach. Two rotary switches with intricate line markings were used to fine-tune the input signal when recording, which activated two vertical strips of LEDs. Across all tape recorder models, a total of 45,000 units were produced.

Also in the series: C 2 (1982), C 3 (1983), C 4 (1987), C 2³ (1988)

P 1, 1980
Record player for the atelier system
Peter Hartwein, Dieter Rams
Braun

11.5 × 44.5 × 37 cm (4½ × 17½ × 14½ in)
5 kg (11 lb)

Sheet steel, plastic, aluminium, acrylic
DM 688

In line with all of Braun's record
players, the P 1 from the atelier series
features a transparent acrylic dust
cover; however, its front edge is
chamfered to mimic the same treat-
ment on the device enclosure. This
simple but striking detail, suggested to
Peter Hartwein by Rams, makes it the
perfect culmination to top the stackable sound system. All controls except
the power button are located on the
chamfered edge of the record player,
immediately below the dust cover.
Across four different models, a total
of 50,000 units were produced.

Also in the series: P 2 and P 3 (1982),
P 4 (1984)

R 1, 1981
Receiver for the atelier system
Peter Hartwein, Dieter Rams
Braun

6.5 × 44.5 × 37 cm (2½ × 17½ × 14½ in)
7.9 kg (17½ lb)

Sheet steel, plastic, aluminium
DM 1,250

Also included in the atelier system was a combined receiver and amplifier, which had a slightly more complex interface than other components in the series. The design of the rotary switches and convex push buttons was largely taken from Braun's slim-line audio series (p. 237). When in use, the large green numbers on the frequency display contrast with the tiny red LED triangles that indicate fine-tuning. As with all of Braun's hi-fi systems made since the 1960s, the power button stands out in green, making it immediately clear how to turn on the device. Braun's last standalone receiver for the atelier series, the R 4 from 1987, was designed to be compatible with other external devices, such as a personal computer. Across the series, 35,000 units of the receiver were produced.

Also in the series: R 2 (1986), R 4 (1987), R 4-2 (1989)

CD 3, 1985 / CD 4, 1986 (pictured)
CD player for the atelier system
Peter Hartwein, Dieter Rams
Braun

6.5 × 44.5 × 37 cm (2½ × 17½ × 14½ in)
8.6 kg (19 lb)

Sheet steel, plastic, aluminium
DM 2,200

The atelier CD player came onto the
market later than the system's other
components, as Braun had to wait for
the technology to be developed.
Similar to the C 1 tape recorder (p. 278),
the device had a motorized tray that
inserted and ejected the CD. Across
five different models, a total of 55,000
units of the CD player were produced.

Also in the series: CD 2 and CD 5
(1988), CD 2³ (1989)

AF 1, 1982
Pedestal stand for the atelier sytem
Dieter Rams
Braun

36 × 37.5 × 25.1 cm (14¼ × 14¾ × 10 in)
3.3 kg (7¾ lb)

Plastic
DM 300

This column-shaped stand allowed
the atelier components to be stacked
up and presented as a free-standing
system. Each of the devices has a
cover on the back to conceal the
wiring, which instead is fed through
the supporting column of the stand
and consolidated in a tube at the
base, meaning the set-up could be
placed anywhere in a room.

LS 60, 1982 / LS 80, 1982 (pictured)
Loudspeaker for the atelier system
Peter Hartwein, Dieter Rams
Braun

37 × 22.5 × 21.5 cm (14½ × 9 × 8½ in)
6.9 kg (15¼ lb)

Wood, aluminium
DM 400

A series of loudspeakers was also
developed for the atelier sound system.
Their distinctive chamfered edges,
which visually aligned them with the
rest of the atelier components, were
mirrored on the loudspeaker grilles.
Rams received a patent for his design
of a grille attachment mechanism, a
groove that allows for easy installation
and removal.

Also in the series: LS 70, LS 100
and LS 120 (1982), LS 150 (1982–7),
LS 40 (1983)

RC 1, 1986
Remote control for the atelier system
Peter Hartwein
Braun

4.4 × 7.8 × 19.5 cm (1¾ × 3 × 7¾ in)
0.25 kg (½ lb)

Plastic
DM 300

The RC 1 universal remote control
was designed for use with the atelier
sound system's later devices. Its
control buttons were matched to the
different functions of each audio
separate. Although such complexity
would not have been appropriate for
the analogue audio industry, the
device is completely self-explanatory
and intuitive to use; 32,000 units of
the remote control were produced.

TV 3, 1986
Colour television for the atelier system
Peter Hartwein, Dieter Rams
Braun

59.2 × 65 × 49 cm (23¼ × 25½ × 19¼ in)
35 kg (77¼ lb)

Plastic
DM 2,700

In 1986, Braun released a television set as part of the atelier sound system. As with all of the company's TV designs, made under the supervision of Rams, the set had a subtly protruding, full-frame picture screen. Unconventionally, the angle of the screen could be adjusted to tilt upwards, allowing the TV to be placed on the floor. A total of 10,000 units of the TV 3 were produced.

dymatic, 1980
Pocket lighter
Dieter Rams
Braun

7.5 × 3 × 1.8 cm (3 × 1¼ × ¾ in)
0.15 kg (¼ lb)

Aluminium, plastic
DM 84

This pocket lighter is a pleasure to hold, as well as having a functional and aesthetically appealing design. The two rectangles that comprise the casing and switch form a striking image. Moreover, the downward motion required to ignite the flame means that the thumb is pulled away from it when lit. The dymatic's successor, the club, had an even slimmer design.

Also in the series: club (1981)

variabel, 1981
Candle lighter
Dieter Rams
Braun

17.5 × 3 × 1.8 cm (7 × 1¼ × ¾ in)
0.25 kg (½ lb)

Aluminium, plastic
DM 155

The dymatic, club and variabel models
were the last three lighters to be
released by Braun. Starting from the
basic shape of the dymatic (opposite),
the form of the variabel was stretched
to make this sophisticated candle lighter.

ET 55 control LCD, 1981
Pocket calculator
Dieter Rams, Dietrich Lubs
Braun

The ET 55 was the first Braun
calculator to be produced in white as
well as the standard black. It remained
in production for six years, the longest
of all Braun pocket calculators.

13.6 × 7.8 × 1 cm (5½ × 3 × ½ in)
0.4 kg (1 lb)

Plastic, acrylic
DM 76

ABR 11, 1981
Clock radio
Dietrich Lubs, Dieter Rams
Braun

As a follow-up to the ABR 21 clock
radio (p. 254–5), Rams and Dietrich
Lubs developed a larger device
using a similar construction but with
a much improved sound. Two metal
bars were installed along the front of
the top edge that turned off the alarm
when pressed. The alarm setting used
twenty-four-hour time so it would
only go off once a day.

15 × 21.5 × 10 cm (6 × 8½ × 4 in)
0.9 kg (2 lb)

Plastic, acrylic
DM 172

Prototype for a torch, 1982
Dieter Rams, Ludwig Littmann
Gillette

18 × 4.3/9 cm in diameter (7 × 1¾/3½ in)
0.35 kg (¾ in)

Plastic, glass
Not released for sale

This torch was developed in collaboration with Gillette's team of engineers based in Boston. It was intended for outdoor use and was lit using a gas mantle and butane cartridge. Due to insufficient means of communication between the two international teams, cooperation turned out to be difficult and the project was never realized.

Heladora IC 1, 1982
Ice-cream maker
Dieter Rams
Braun Española

12 × 27.5 × 16.5 cm (4¾ × 10¾ × 6½ in)
0.9 kg (2 lb)

Plastic, acrylic
Price unknown

Ice-cream making has a special significance in Spain. This appliance, designed in collaboration with Braun Española's engineering team, made it possible for consumers to make professional-quality ice cream at home. Once the ice cream is mixed, the internal container can be removed and chilled in the freezer. The bowl, mixing arm and power unit combine in a clean geometric design.

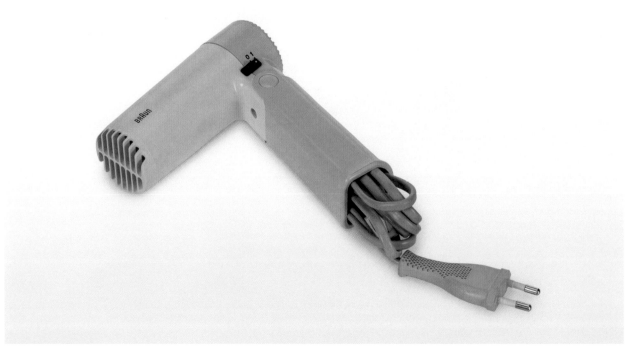

Secudor Pistola PG-700, 1983
Travel hair dryer
Dieter Rams, Robert Oberheim
Braun Española

15.5 × 12.8 × 4.8 cm (6 × 5 × 2 in)
0.25 kg (½ lb)

Plastic
Price unknown

This travel hair dryer, developed with
Braun Española's engineering team
for the Spanish market, reflects the
design of the compact 1000 made
by Robert Oberheim in the Kronberg
headquarters in the same year.
However, the Spanish model has
a slightly larger handle, which, similar
to Oberheim's design, can be used
to stow the cord.

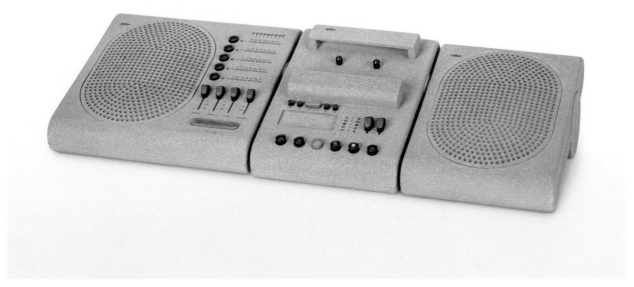

Prototype for a clock radio with
cassette player accessory, 1982
Dieter Rams, Dietrich Lubs
Braun

For a clock radio to have significantly
high sound quality, it requires a
large loudspeaker. For this prototype,
the oval speaker grille was borrowed
from the L 308 loudspeakers (p. 200)
and is flanked by a series of slide
controls and push buttons. The lectern-
shaped unit could also be paired with
a matching cassette player, so that the
user could be woken by their choice
of song.

9.3 × 16.2/23.2 × 22.5 cm (3¾ × 6½/9
× 8¾ in)
0.13–0.17 kg (¼–½ lb)

Plastic
Not released for sale

Lufthansa competition, 1983
Prototypes for in-flight tableware
Braun design team, Dieter Rams
Lufthansa

Various sizes and weights

Plastic, porcelain
Not released for sale

In 1983, Rams and his design department were invited to take part in a
competition to redesign Lufthansa's
in-flight tableware. The intention with
this exercise was for the team to take
on more external commissions in the
future. Their only rival was the designer
Wolf Karnagel, who ultimately won
the competition.

The Braun team designed numerous
products, from salt shakers to coffee
pots, and a variety of different recep-
tacles. Of particular note was the
design of a porcelain cup, which drew
on ideas that Rams had developed
eight years earlier (p. 216); its heat-
resistant plastic handle allowed for
safe handling.

Prototype for a razor, 1983
Dieter Rams, Jürgen Greubel
Gillette

23.3 × 12 × 4 cm (9¼ × 4¾ × 1½ in)
0.02 kg (¾ oz)

Plastic
Not released for sale

As an alternative to the octagon razor
(opposite), Rams and Jürgen Greubel
proposed several other suggestions.
This design features a series of
graphic grooves along the handle.

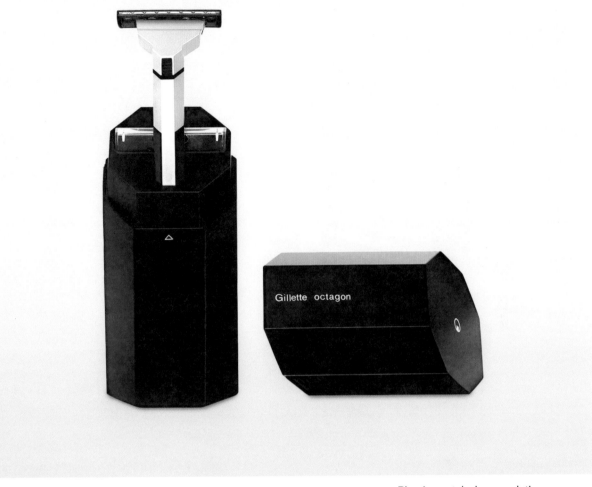

Gillette octagon, 1983
Prototype for a premium razor and
packaging
Dieter Rams, Jürgen Greubel

Gillette
Size and weight unknown

Plastic, metal, chrome plating
Not released for sale

In 1983, Gillette commissioned the
Braun design team to create a
high-quality razor. For their proposal,
Rams and Jürgen Greubel put forward
a design for an octagonal black handle
with a striking chrome finish at both
ends; the handle itself was to be made
of die-cast metal. In contrast to
lightweight plastic razors, those with
greater weight are much more efficient
and comfortable to use as they do not
have to be pressed against the skin.
Rams and Greubel's design featured a
striated grip, which would have added
further to its sturdy feel. Precious
woods, polished horn or mother-of-
pearl were offered in place of the
standard plastic razor head, reinforcing
the premium feel of the product, and

the designers packaged the whole
thing in an elaborate octagonal case.
A small triangle indicates where the
two-part box should be pulled open;
the flat surface of the lid slants
forward, creating a platform on which
the Gillette logo is discreetly printed,
a solution devised by the Braun
graphic design department headed
by Wolfgang Schmittel.

Paravent, 1984
Room divider
Dieter Rams, Marcello Morandini
Rosenthal

175 × 65/100 × 3 cm (69 × 25½/39½
× 1¼ in)
approx. 10 kg (22 lb)

Laminated wood
Price unknown

Rams was commissioned by porcelain and household goods company Rosenthal to create the basic framework for a room divider, which would then be elaborated on by the Italian artist and graphic designer Marcello Morandini. The project was initiated by Philip Rosenthal, son and heir of Philipp Rosenthal, the company's founder, who had a particular interest in art and embarked on a number of artist collaboration projects during his time as CEO. This design marked a time when the company was looking to enter the furniture market. Rams's submission comprised only the main structure of the three-panelled room divider, after which several Rosenthal artists and designers submitted artwork suggestions; Morandini's proposal was the only one that Rams found acceptable. The Paravent was produced in a limited edition of twenty-five signed and numbered units.

AB 2, 1984
Alarm clock
Jürgen Greubel, Dieter Rams
Braun

9.2 × 7.5 × 3.5 cm (3½ × 3 × 1½ in)
0.05 kg (1¾ oz)

Plastic, acrylic
DM 29.95

The AB 2 alarm clock by Rams and
Jürgen Greubel was inspired by
the form of a classic table clock,
but reproduced in plastic. With its
distinctive feet and familiar Braun
dial, the AB 2 was available in nine
different colours.

KF 40, 1984
Coffee maker
Hartwig Kahlcke
Braun / De'Longhi

30.7 × 17.5 × 23 cm (12 × 7 × 9 in)
1.6 kg (3½ lb)

Plastic, glass
DM 70

In 1984, twelve years after the release of the KF 20 coffee maker (pp. 190–1), Hartwig Kahlcke followed up with the KF 40, a design that is still in production today, sold under the name KF 47/1 by Braun/De'Longhi. The water tank is now directly connected to the base, and so requires only one heating system. Its two stacked cylinders play on the KF 20's tower-like construction, although the resulting form is squatter than its predecessor. Functional and easy to use, the coffee maker's upper filter section can be opened out and the filter changed. The rear of the water reservoir is lined with moulded vertical striations, which help give structure to the expansive surface area. Another distinctive feature is the semi-circular carafe handle, which is intersected by an internal bar, making it easier to grip and manoeuvre; its open form also saves on material and results in a lighter appearance. With its timeless aesthetic and improved design, the KF 40 has spawned many replicas throughout the industry.

Also in the series: KF 45 (1984)

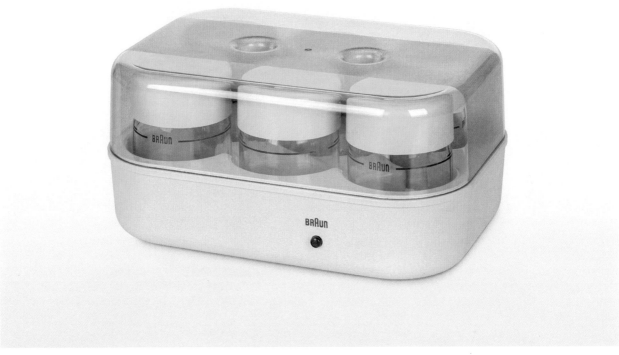

Yogurtera YG-1, 1984
Yoghurt machine
Dieter Rams, Ludwig Littmann
Braun Española

This yoghurt maker, largely designed
by the engineering department at
Braun Española, was only available on
the Spanish market. The large, white,
rounded-edged lids visually integrate
the pots into the appliance.

12.5 × 21 × 21 cm (5 × 8¼ × 8¼ in)
0.7 kg (1½ lb)

Plastic
Price unknown

Prototype for a coffee maker, 1985
Dieter Rams, Jürgen Greubel
Braun

30.5 × 32.5 × 18 cm (12 × 12¾ × 7 in)
5 kg (11 lb)

Plastic, acrylic
Not released for sale

Compared to Hartwig Kahlcke's KF 40
design (p. 300), this prototype for a
coffee maker has a more conventional
layout, with a water reservoir on the
left and a matching carafe and filter on
the right. The two elements are
connected to each other via a striking
red tube, resulting in a form that is both
sophisticated and pictorial. The coffee
maker was intended to be mounted on
a wall using a bracket.

AB 46 24h, 1985
Alarm clock
Dietrich Lubs, Dieter Rams
Braun

This alarm clock features a large on/
off button on the top and a twenty-
four-hour time function with which to
set the alarm.

9 × 7.5 × 3.5 cm (3½ × 3 × 1½ cm)
0.1 kg (¼ lb)

Plastic, acrylic
DM 62.50

850, 1986
Conference table programme
Dieter Rams
Vitsœ / sdr+

Various sizes and weights

Laminated blockboard, aluminium
DM 909–2,126

This long conference table could be assembled with either a rectangular or oval table top, which was divided into segments for easier transport. The unusual positioning of the aluminium legs towards the centre of the table enabled people to sit comfortably without being disturbed. However, in order to provide sufficient stability, the table legs were filled with waste metal shavings. This innovative design, first produced by Vitsœ and later by Cologne-based furniture company sdr+ (systemmöbel dieter rams), was adopted by other manufacturers. Indeed, sdr+ later varied the table legs without consulting Rams, which contributed to the cooling of the designer's relationship with the brand.

862, 1986
Armchair
Dieter Rams, Jürgen Greubel
Vitsœ

82 × 64 × 60 cm (32¼ × 25¼ × 23½ in)
9 kg (19¾ lb)

Aluminium, plastic, wood; textile or
leather upholstery
DM 1,427–1,740 (prices from 1988)

The structure of the 862 armchair
comprises bent metal tubing, which
forms the front legs, arm rests and
backrest support, rear legs in ash and
a wooden crossmember at the front;
the upholstered seat and backrest
are assembled in between. Another
version of the armrests was available
with wide, padded leather cushioning.
Specifically designed to use with the
850 conference table (opposite), the
chair had special attention paid to its
ergonomics in order to achieve a good
seating position.

exact universal, 1986
Beard trimmer
Roland Ullmann
Braun

With its clean, rectangular shape,
and technical and visual longevity,
the exact universal beard trimmer
by Roland Ullmann can still be
appreciated today.

16 × 4 × 3 cm (6¼ × 1½ × 1¼ in)
0.17 kg (½ lb)

Plastic
DM 139

dual aqua, c.1986
Preliminary shaver design
Dieter Rams, Roland Ullmann
Braun

Due to the company's increasingly
successful sales in Japan, in the
mid-1980s Braun began work on an
electric shaver designed specifically
to serve this market. The motor was
housed in a narrow plastic enclosure
with a minimal grey and black colour
scheme. In early consumer tests,
the design did not prove a hit with the
target male audience. However, the
slim design found later success as
the Lady Braun style of 1988 (p. 315).
The name 'dual aqua' refers to the
fact that the shaver can be rinsed
under running water.

13.3 × 5 × 2.6 cm (5¼ × 2 × 1 in)
0.16 kg (½ lb)

Plastic
Not released for sale

PDC silencio 1200 travel set, 1986
Travel hair dryer with accessories
Robert Oberheim
Braun

16 × 15 × 7 cm (6¼ × 6 × 2¾ in)
0.35 kg (¾ lb)

Plastic
DM 63.50

Intended to cater to the well-groomed
traveller, the silencio 1200 travel set
came with a number of different
accessories, including a hair dryer, an
iron, a spray bottle and a plastic bag
that could be used to dry clothes. It
symbolizes a more arduous approach
to global travel, once a novelty for the
majority of people; today there is a
hair dryer in practically every hotel
bathroom, albeit sporting a handle that
is more or less modelled on Braun's
classic angled design.

AB 1, 1987
Alarm clock
Dietrich Lubs
Braun

6.3 × 6.3 × 3.7 cm (2½ × 2½ × 1½ in)
0.04 kg (1½ oz)

Plastic
DM 24.95

This small and inexpensive alarm clock has a Minimalist design consisting only of a narrow box, whose front surface is almost entirely covered by the dial. No other features distract from Braun's signature graphic design: white hour and minute hands paired with white numerals and a wafer-thin, yellow second hand set against a black background. Only a single Braun logo is placed on the dial; none can be seen on the enclosure itself – the company's alarm clocks were now so distinctive that this additional branding was no longer necessary. All of Braun's analogue alarm clocks used the same unobtrusive tone, making them instantly recognizable to the trained ear.

ST 1 solar card, 1987
Credit card-sized calculator
Dietrich Lubs
Braun

5.5 × 8.5 × 0.3 cm (2¼ × 3¼ × 1/8 in)
0.02 kg (¾ oz)

Plastic
DM 29.95

Dietrich Lubs recalls creating the
design of this ultra-slim pocket
calculator as he hurriedly sketched it
on the edge of a bed in his hotel room;
the Chinese manufacturer was in a
rush and wanted to see his proposal
right away. The technology and overall
form of the ST 1 solar drew on existing
Braun devices, but the layout, adapted
to fit the new credit-card size, sets it
apart from its predecessors.

ET 66 control, 1987
Pocket calculator
Dietrich Lubs, Dieter Rams
Braun

13.7 × 7.7 × 1.3 cm (5½ × 3 × ½ in)
0.09 kg (¼ lb)

Plastic, acrylic
DM 59.50

Of all the Braun calculators, the ET 66 control has the most well-balanced design; it was also one of the cheapest to buy. The omission of the slide switch from the preceding ET 55 model (p. 288) reduced surface ornamentation to only the recessed display and flat buttons, whose colour scheme was now perfected: the numbers are in black; the arithmetic operations in brown; and the memory functions in dark green. This was further complemented by the green and red of the on and off switches, and the eye-catching yellow of the equals sign button. Blue was deliberately left out of the palette, as Rams and Dietrich Lubs felt that using all three primary colours would have made the device too colourful.

As a tribute to the designers' now-iconic creation, Jonathan Ive based the appearance of the calculator app on the first Apple iPhone on the ET 66 calculator. Since 2013, the ET 66 has been distributed by the English company Zeon, under the Braun brand, using the name BNE001BK.

rgs 1 (fsb 1138), 1987–8
Door handle programme
Dieter Rams
FSB

4 × 14.2 × 6.4 cm (1½ × 5½ × 2½ in)
0.17 kg (½ lb)

Die-cast aluminium, thermoplastic
DM 135 per pair

Even something as seemingly simple as a door handle can pose a challenge for designers. In 1986, the German manufacturer FSB held a design competition and invited nine renowned architects and designers to take part: Hans-Ulrich Bitsch, Mario Botta, Peter Eisenman, Shoji Hayashi, Hans Hollein, Arata Isozaki, Alessandro Mendini, Dieter Rams and Petr Tucny. Rams's submission comprised three practical and semantically appealing designs, which were produced by FSB until the end of the 2000s. The rgs 1 (the letters 'rgs' being the German initials for 'Rams', 'grey' and 'black') was the most successful. The prominent silver circle is the most important design element, symbolizing rotation, i.e. the basic function of a handle. The aluminium lever is lined with thermoplastic on the front and back, providing a comfortable fit for the hand; and the indentation on the underside of the lever provides a natural resting place for the index finger so that the handle can be gripped firmly. Following the competition, Rams extended his door handle programme to include a total of twenty-seven designs, which, aside from the first three models, includes window handles, keyhole covers, signs, a number of custom models, a cabinet handle and a door stopper. In 1996, the architect Christoph Ingenhoven fitted out the entirety of his 127-m (417-ft) -tall, thirty-storey RWE Tower in Essen with rgs 1 handles.

rgs 2 (fsb 1136), 1987–8
Door handle programme
Dieter Rams, Angela Knoop
FSB

Rams's second door handle, the
rgs 2, was made in collaboration with
Angela Knoop, who worked with Rams
in the FSB design workshop. Knoop
created the basic shape, while Rams
worked on the details, adding a subtle
index finger recess behind the
lever head.

2.8 × 13 × 6.5 cm (1 × 5 × 2½ in)
0.18 kg (½ lb)

Die-cast aluminium, thermoplastic
DM 110 per pair

rgs 3 (fsb 1137), 1987–8
Door handle programme
Dieter Rams, Angela Knoop
FSB

The third door handle that Rams
produced is bent into an elegant
U-shape, and, like the preceding
models, is made of aluminium and
black thermoplastic. A small recess
was also added on the inside of the
handle for the little finger to rest on.

2.8 × 14 × 6.5 cm (1 × 5½ × 2½ in)
0.19 kg (½ lb)

Die-cast aluminium, thermoplastic
DM 110 per pair

Lady Braun style, 1988
Women's shaver
Roland Ullmann
Braun

This electric shaver was designed
specifically for women. Its very narrow
motor unit and battery compartment
are housed in the handle.

15.5 × 5.5 × 2.7 cm (6 × 2 × 1 in)
0.4 kg (1 lb)

Plastic
DM 89

Prototypes for a pillar clock, 1988
Dieter Rams, Dietrich Lubs
Förderverein Schöneres Frankfurt e.V.

37.4 × 8.8 × 7.7 cm (14¾ × 3½ × 3 in)
0.7 kg (1½ lb)

Plastic, metal
Not released for sale

The Förderverein Schöneres Frankfurt e.V. was a society founded in 1977 by the citizens of Frankfurt to help with the beautification of the city. With support from Volker Fischer, a design curator at the Museum Angewandte Kunst (Museum of Applied Arts), Frankfurt am Main, and designer Matthias Dietz, the association held a competition in 1988 for the design of a series of pillar clocks that could be installed in public spaces around the city. A total of twenty-three architects, designers and sculptors were invited to enter, including Volker Albus, Konstantin Grcic, Herbert Lindinger, Michele De Lucchi, Martin Székély, Hannes Wettstein and, of course, Dieter Rams. In collaboration with

Dietrich Lubs, Rams designed a three-sided monolithic tower clock clad in silver, atlas grey or black sheet steel; it featured an analogue dial on each side, the design of which was based on previous Braun models. They also put forward one version with a solar-powered clock. Ultimately, Martin Székély and Hannes Wettstein won the competition, so Rams and Lubs's designs were never realized.

AW 10, 1989
Wristwatch
Dietrich Lubs
Braun

0.65 × 3.3 cm in diameter (¼ × 1¼ in)
0.02 kg (¾ oz)

Plastic, metal, aluminium, acrylic,
leather
DM 130

Following the release of Rams's first digital watches in the late 1970s, the DW 20 (p. 240) and DW 30 (p. 252), Dietrich Lubs embarked on the design of an analogue watch, which surpassed all successive models in terms of clarity. Featuring Braun's characteristic graphic purism, the dial of the AW 10 was surrounded by a plastic bezel to protect it from scuffs and marks caused by shirt cuffs and trouser pockets.

The incentive to design an analogue watch came from Braun's sales team, who had previously applied the Braun logo to existing designs to use as promotional gifts for clients. The challenge was to create something that was in line with Braun's high aesthetic values while also offering the perfect branding opportunity. The AW 10 inspired a whole series of high-quality Braun analogue wristwatches.

Also in the series: AW 15 (1994)

Gillette Sensor, 1989
Razor
Dieter Rams, Jürgen Greubel
Gillette

13 × 4 × 2.2 cm (5 × 1½ × 1 in)
0.03 kg (1 oz)

Metal-coated plastic, metal
US$ 3.75

In the late 1980s, Gillette developed a groundbreaking new razor blade system and commissioned the Braun design team to create the handle. Its plastic body was covered with a thin layer of silver metal and featured black plastic lateral ridges for grip, creating an effect similar to that used on Braun's micron shaver range (p. 265). To market the new system, Gillette required a master branding strategy and proceeded to invest US$200 million in its development and advertising. In 1990, the razor featured during the most expensive advertising event in the United States, the twenty-fourth Super Bowl. However, it more than paid for itself: the Braun-designed Sensor became the world's most successful razor, with twenty-one million units sold within the first six months.

1990–2020

ABR 313 sl, 1990
Alarm clock radio
Dietrich Lubs
Braun

7 × 15.5 × 2.4 cm (2¾ × 6 × 1 in)
0.2 kg (½ lb)

Plastic, acrylic
DM 119

This small travel alarm clock radio
features the typical Braun dial,
but extends widthways to include
a loudspeaker on the right and a
chamfered side panel on the left,
on which the tuning and volume
adjustment dials are placed.

flex control 4515, 1990 /
4520 universal, 1990 (pictured)
Electric shaver
Roland Ullmann

Braun
13 × 5.2 × 2.7 cm (5 × 2 × 1 in)
0.3 kg (¾ lb)

Plastic or aluminium, metal
DM 289

The flex control 4515, designed by
Roland Ullmann in collaboration
with Braun technicians, featured a
pivoting, twin-foil head that adjusted
to the contours of the face, providing
a particularly close shave. Its tactile
studded surface was transferred from
the micron razor series (p. 265).

Also in the series: flex control 4550
universal cc (1991)

AW 50, 1991
Wristwatch
Dieter Rams, Dietrich Lubs
Braun

Although Braun watches were
predominantly designed by Dietrich
Lubs, Rams was directly involved in
the design of this particular model.
Following the basic shape of the AW 10
(p. 317), the clock face on the AW 50
was made entirely of metal, including
its rounded bezel. The designers also
added a date display.

4.5 × 0.5 × 3.2 cm in diameter (1¾ × ¼
× 1¼ in)
0.04 kg (1½ oz)

Metal, aluminium, acrylic, leather
DM 375

ET 88 world traveller, 1991
Pocket calculator
Dietrich Lubs, Dieter Rams
Braun

13.7 × 7.7 × 1.1 cm (5½ × 3 × ½ in)
0.1 kg (¼ lb)

Plastic, acrylic
DM 119

Braun's last pocket calculator was
intended as a travel companion and
included a digital clock and world
time function. The hinged flap that
protected the screen while stowed
featured a diagram of world time
zones; instead of Berlin, Frankfurt was
used to represent Germany, as was
the case with all of Braun's travel alarm
clocks. The flap can also be folded
back to prop up the calculator when in
use. Braun engineers were intensively
involved in developing this aspect
of a design that was otherwise
produced in the Far East.

DB 10 sl, 1991
Alarm clock
Dietrich Lubs, Dieter Rams
Braun

9.5 × 8 × 8.5 cm (3¾ × 3 × 3¼ in)
0.16 kg (½ lb)

Plastic, acrylic
DM 179 (DB 10 fsl)

This alarm clock was designed as a right-angled triangular prism. The front is divided into two parts: the digital display at the top and a keypad for the settings at the bottom. Each function has its own control button, making operation straightforward. The keypad is protected by a cover flap when not in use, inside which the operating instructions are printed. The extraordinarily shaped device was offered in both digital quartz and radio-controlled versions. The later DB 12 fsl features a temperature display.

Also in the series: DB 10 fsl (1991), DB 12 fsl temperature (1996)

RHa 1/2, 1998
Desk lamp
Dieter Rams, Andreas Hackbarth
Tecnolumen

Pole: 64.5 × 63 × 1.2–1.4 cm in diameter
(25½ × 24¾ × ½ in); shade: 8 × 10.7 cm
in diameter (3 × 4¼ in); rail:
12 × 70 × 16.5 cm (4¾ × 27½ × 6½ in)
With transformer: 4 kg (8¾ lb)

Aluminium, steel, plastic
DM 567–764

In 1981, Andreas Hackbarth, a
postgraduate student mentored
by Rams at the Hochschule für
bildende Künste (University of Fine
Arts) Hamburg, prepared his thesis
on a desk lamp. While on a work
placement at Braun the following year,
he developed a design prototype in
collaboration with Rams, resulting
in the RHa 1/2 lamp. The design is
supported by a U-profile base affixed
to two stainless steel, desk-mounted
rods, along which it can be moved.
This U-profile acts as a holder for the
adjustable stand, as well as housing
the transformer and the power switch.
The horizontal section of the lamp
stand can be swivelled 180 degrees.
In another possible set-up, the
U-profile can be mounted directly
to the desk.

In 1995, the design was published
in Rams's book *Weniger, aber
besser* (*Less, But Better*), which
aroused the interest of German
lighting manufacturer Tecnolumen.
After a further reworking by Rams
and Hackbarth, as well as the
company's lighting engineers, the
lamp was presented at the Euroluce
International Lighting Exhibition in
Milan in April 1998.

329

Gift bowl for Expo 2000 Hannover,
1998
Dieter Rams
Fürstenberg / FSB

13.2 × 7.5/21 cm in diameter
(5¼ × 3/8¼ in)
1.72 kg (3¾ lb)

Porcelain, metal, wood
Not released for sale

For the World's Fair Expo 2000, held in Hannover, Rams designed a limited edition gift bowl, which was given to all participating countries by the organizers. It consisted of three nested porcelain bowls and a stainless steel holder in the shape of a quarter hemisphere. The stacked cylindrical base was made of porcelain, maple and metal discs, which Rams chose to represent the Expo motto 'Mankind, Nature, Technology, Creating a New World'. The outer, greenish-brown, hemispherical porcelain bowl symbolized the earth; the black and white inner porcelain bowls stood for human diversity; and the metal holder represented technology. The bowl was manufactured in two parts, with

Fürstenberg creating the porcelain components and FSB the metal elements. Only 250 units were made.

4000 RA 98, 1998
Stacking chair
Dieter Rams
Kusch+Co

83 × 53 × 65 cm (32¾ × 21 × 25½ in)
7–8.5 kg (15½–18¾ lb)

Chrome plated tubular steel, powder-coated aluminium, natural or stained beech, fabric upholstery (optional)
DM 488–950

The 4000 RA 98 stacking chair featured an ergonomically designed shell on a cast iron framework connected to four tubular steel legs. Rams originally planned for the front legs to be made of die-cast aluminium, as shown in the image, but the manufacturer opted for the more cost-effective steel. The chair was only produced in small numbers.

Nesting table programme 010, 2001
Nesting tables
Dieter Rams, Thomas Merkel
sdr+

Large: 40 × 54.5 × 36 cm
(15¾ × 21½ × 14¼ in);
small: 33.5 × 41.5 × 36 cm
(13¼ × 16¼ × 14¼ in)
Large: 6 kg (13¼ lb); small: 5 kg (11 lb)

Powder-coated aluminium
Large: DM 200.68–307.40; small:
DM 189.08–266 (prices from 2002)

These heavy nesting tables are made
from 5-mm (¼-in) -thick aluminium,
which curves – outwards for the
smaller table and inwards for the larger
table – 90 degrees at the base,
allowing the two forms to join perfectly
together. When the tables sit flush with
one another, the gap between them
can be used to store newspapers and
magazines. In a longer version of the
design, the lower table also serves
as a bench seat and comes with a felt
cover. The nesting tables were
developed as an alternative to the 621
model from 1962 (p. 97), which sdr+ did
not want to re-release due to its high
tooling costs.

Tsatsas 931, 2018
Ladies' handbag
Dieter Rams
Tsatsas

17 × 24.5 × 6.5 cm (6¾ × 9½ × 2½ in)
0.47 kg (1 lb)

Calfskin and lamb nappa leather
€900 (price from 2020)

In 2018, the small Frankfurt leather goods label Tsatsas released a handbag that Rams first designed in the 1960s. Through his early work on leather cases for Braun shavers and other small appliances, Rams had come into contact with a local bag making company in Offenbach. However, the design was never intended for mass production, but exclusively as gifts for his wife Ingeborg and some close friends. Even when working on personal projects, and with products he had less experience with, Rams was interested in the qualities of the material and the workmanship involved.

606, 2020
Wall-mounted desk
Dieter Rams
Vitsœ

73.5/104 × 120–180 × 65.5/90 cm
(29/41 × 47¼–71 × 25¾–35½ in)
Various weights

Plywood
Pricing not yet available

In 2018, Rams reworked the design
of the wall-mounted desk unit for
the 606 Universal Shelving System
(pp. 65–9). Rather than using an all-
over lamination, the layered wood desk
is exposed on the sides, providing
a pleasing contrast to the white or
black surface finish. The front and side
edges were chamfered to give the
desk a more elegant appearance.

BIBLIOGRAPHY

Editorial note: in the following bibliography the magazine *Design+Design* (1984–2011) is always listed under this title. However, the original title of issue no. 1 (printed and published independently in 1984, with a print run of 100 copies, by Klaus Rudolph in Hannover) to no. 7 was *Der Braun Sammler;* from issue no. 8 to no. 21, the title was *Braun+Design*.

GENERAL LITERATURE BY AND ABOUT DIETER RAMS

Aldersey-Williams, Hugh, 'Modern Masters: Dieter Rams', *I.D.,* 36, no. 5 (1989), 32–5.

Burkhardt, Francois, 'Future Prospects and Utopian Ideas', interview with Dieter Rams (1980), in *Design and Art,* ed. Alex Coles. (London and Cambridge, Mass., 2007), 114–16.

Burkhardt, Francois, and Inez Franksen (eds), *Design: Dieter Rams* (Berlin, 1980).

De Jong, Cees W. (ed.), *Zehn Thesen für gutes Design – Dieter Rams* (*Ten Principles for Good Design – Dieter Rams*) (Munich, 2017).

———, *Diteo Ramseu* (Dieter Rams) (Seoul, 2018).

Domdey, Andreas, *Mehr oder Weniger: Braun Design im Vergleich (More or Less: Braun Design in Comparison),* exhibition catalogue, Museum für Kunst und Gewerbe, Hamburg (Hamburg, 1990).

Düchting, Hajo, *50 Designer, die man kennen sollte* (*50 Designers Everybody Should Know*) (Munich, 2012).

Feireiss, Lukas, *Legacy: Generations of Creatives in Dialogue* (Amsterdam, 2018).

Feltrup, Sergio, and Agustín Trabucco, *Reflexiones sobre el Diseño Industrial contemporáneo: El ser de los objetos, una visión multidisciplinar* (*Reflections on Contemporary Industrial Design: The Existence of Objects, A Multidisciplinary Vision*) (Buenos Aires, 2014).

Fiell, Charlotte and Peter, 'Dieter Rams', in *Design des 20. Jahrhunderts* (*Twentieth-Century Design*) (Cologne, 2000), 591–3.

———, 'Dieter Rams', in *Industrie-Design A–Z* (*A–Z of Industrial Design*) (Cologne, 2006), 411–13.

Fischer, Volker, *'Dieter Rams', in Design heute: Maßstäbe, Formgebung zwischen Industrie und Kunst-Stück* (*Design Today: Standards and Style Between Industry and Art*), ed. Volker Fischer, exhibition catalogue, Deutsches Architekturmuseum, Frankfurt am Main (Munich, 1988), 125–48.

Hesse, Petra and René Spitz, System Design: Über 100 Jahre Chaos im Alltag (*System Design: Over 100 Years of Chaos in Everyday Life*), exhibition catalogue, Museum für Angewandte Kunst, Cologne (Cologne, 2015).

Hodge, Susie, *When Design Really Works* (New York, 2014).

Jatzke-Wigand, Hartmut, 'Zu diesen Entwürfen stehe ich noch heute' ('I'm Still Sticking to My Design'), interview with Dieter Rams, in *Design+Design,* no. 33 (1995), 6–7.

Judah, Hettie, *We Are Wanderful: 25 Years of Design & Fashion in Limburg* (Tielt, Belgium, 2016).

Klatt, Jo, 'Algo de Braun: Eine kleine Auswahl von Braun Produkten, die im Werk Barcelona hergestellt wurden' ('A Bit of Braun: A Small Selection of Braun Products Manufactured at the Barcelona Factory'), *Design+Design,* no. 88 (2009), 4–7. [see images: p. 291, 292, 301]

Klatt, Jo and Hartmut Jatzke-Wigand (eds), *Möbel-Systeme von Dieter Rams* (*Modular Furniture Systems by Dieter Rams*) (Hamburg, 2002). [see images: pp. 27, 28, 29, 62, 63, 64, 70–1, 90–1, 92–3, 94, 95, 96, 97, 150, 151, 158–9, 181, 195, 210–11, 304]

Klatt, Jo, and Günter Staeffler (eds), *Braun+Design Collection: 40 Jahre Braun –Design 1955 bis 1995* (*Braun+Design Collection: 40 Years of Braun Design – 1955 to 1995*), 2nd edn (Hamburg, 1995).

Klemp, Klaus, 'Dieter Rams trifft Nikolai Petrovich Sheremetev' ('Dieter Rams Meets Nikolai Petrovich Sheremetev'), in *Design: Dieter Rams,* exhibition catalogue, State Museum of Ceramics, Kuskovo Estate, Moscow (Moscow, 2007), 2–29.

———, 'Dieter Rams: Ethics and Modern Philosophy, What Legacy Today?', *docomomo,* no. 46, (2012), 68–75.

———, *Design in Frankfurt: 1920–1990* (Stuttgart, 2014).

———, 'Mid-century Product Design in Germany', in *Mid-Century Modern Complete,* ed. Dominic Bradbury (London, 2014), 278–83.

———, 'Produkt und Protest: Design in Frankfurt in den Sechzigerjahren' ('Product and Protest: Design in Frankfurt in the Sixties'), in *Frankfurt 1960–1969,* ed. Wilhelm E. Opatz (Salenstein, Switzerland, 2016), 100–9.

Klemp, Klaus, and Keiko Ueki-Polet (eds), *Less and More: The Design Ethos of Dieter Rams* (Berlin, 2015).

Komachi, Hanae, 'Dieter Rams', interview with Dieter Rams, in *Axis,* no. 105 (2003), 81–5.

Kozel, Nina, Design: *The Groundbreaking Moments* (Munich, 2013).

Lovell, Sophie, 'Dieter Rams', *Wallpaper,* no. 103 (2007), 317–39.

———, *Dieter Rams: As Little Design as Possible* (London, 2011).

———, *Dieter Rams: So wenig Design wie möglich* (*Dieter Rams: As Little Design as Possible*), (Hamburg, 2013).

McGuirk, Justin, 'Less But Better', *Domus,* no. 887 (2005), 108.

Moss, Richard, 'Braun Style', *Industrial Design,* no. 11 (1962), 36–47; German translation by H. Osthoff and K. Rudolph, *Design+Design,* no. 5 (1986), 22–9.

Mukai, Shutaro, 'Principles of Modern Design and Braun', *Axis,* no. 119 (2006), 164.

Pfaender, Heinz G., and Wilhelm Wagenfeld, *Meine Zeit in der Werkstatt Wagenfeld: Tagebuch 1954– 1957* (*My Time at the Wagenfeld Studio: Diary 1954–1957) (Hamburg, 1998).* [see images: p. 30]

Rams, Dieter, 'Kann Design zum Erfolg eines Unternehmens beitragen?' ('Can Design Contribute to a Company's Success?'), *Werk-Architese, Zeitschrift und Schriftenreihe für Architektur und Kunst,* no. 4 (1977), 9–15.

———, 'Die Rolle des Designers im Industrieunternehmen' ('The Role of the Designer in Industrial Enterprises'), in *Design ist unsichtbar* (*Design is Invisible*), ed. Helmuth Gsöllpointner (Vienna, 1981), 493–506.

———, 'Ramsification', *Designer* (1987), 24.

———, 'Funktionales Design ist eine Zukunftsaufgabe' ('Functional Design is a Mission for the Future'), in *Design Dasein,* exhibition catalogue, Museum für Kunst und Gewerbe, Hamburg (Hamburg, 1987), 155–9.

———, 'Functional Design: A Challenge for the Future?', *Tools 3,* no. 3 (1987): 14–15.

———, 'Erinnerungen an die ersten Jahre bei Braun' ('Memories of the First Years at Braun'), in *Johannes Potente, Brakel: Design der 50er Jahre* (*Johannes Potente, Brakel: Design of the 1950s*), ed. Otl Aicher et al. (Cologne, 1989), 70–6.

———, 'Technologie Design', *design report,* no. 12 (1989), 36–41.

———, 'Beyond the Logic of Consumerism', *Ottagono,* no. 102 (1992), 22–9.

———, 'Ten Principles for Good Design', *Domus,* no. 748 (1993), 21–8.

———, 'Fremtidens Design' ('Design of the Future'), *Design DK,* no. 5 (1995), 37–44.

———, 'Omit the Unimportant', in *The Industrial Design Reader,* ed. Carma Gorman (New York, 2003), 208–11.

———, 'Die Verantwortung des Designs' ('The Responsibility of Design'), in *Im Designerpark: Leben in künstlichen Welten* (*In the Designer Park: Life in Artificial Worlds*), ed. Kai Buchholz, exhibition catalogue, Institut Mathildenhöhe, Darmstadt (Darmstadt, Germany, 2004), 106–13.

———, *Weniger, aber besser* (*Less, but Better*), 5th edn (Berlin, 2014).

Rams, Dieter, and Uta Brandes, *Die leise Ordnung der Dinge* (*The Quiet Order of Things*) (Göttingen: 1990).

Rams, Dieter, and Joe Dolce, 'Master's Choice', *I.D.,* 34, no. 5 (1987), 46–8.

Rams, Dieter, and Reinhard Komar, *Auf der Suche nach dem Morgen: Weniger, aber Besser, Statement für ein Grünes Bauhaus* (*In Search of Tomorrow: Less but Better, Statement for a Green Bauhaus*) (Oldenburg, Germany, 2011).

Schaff, Milton, *Designing the Modern: Profiles of Modernist Designers* (2015).

Schauer, Ute, and Michael Schneider, *Dieter Rams Design: Die Faszination des Einfachen* (*Dieter Rams Design: The Fascination of the Simple*), exhibition catalogue, Institut für Neue Technische Form, Darmstadt (Darmstadt, Germany, 2002).

Schönwandt, Rudolf, '25 Jahre Dieter Rams & Braun-Design' ('25 Years Dieter Rams & Braun-Design') *form,* no. 91 (1980), 20–3.

Scott Jeffries, Samantha, and Grant Scott, 'Less, but Better', *At Home with the Makers of Style* (London, 2005), 176–83.

Shimokawa, Miki (ed.), *Weniger aber besser: Die Welt von Dieter Rams* (*Less but Better: The World of Dieter Rams*) (Kyoto and Frankfurt am Main, 2005).

———, *East Meets West: Urushi-Lack und Design (Ettore Sottsass, Dieter Rams, Fritz Frenkler),* exhibition catalogue, Die Neue Sammlung, The Design Museum, Munich (Munich, 2012).

Sparke, Penny, 'Dieter Rams', in *A Century of Design: Design Pioneers of the 20th Century* (London, 1998), 184–7.

——— et al., *Industrial Design in the Modern Age* (New York, 2018).

Terstiege, Gerrit, 'Der Systematiker'

('The Systematist'), *form*, no. 183 (2002), 76–81.

———, 'Schneewittchen und die sieben Designer' ('Snow White and the Seven Designers'), *form*, no. 207 (2006), 34.

Vitra Design Museum (ed.), *Atlas des Möbeldesigns* (*Atlas of Furniture Design*) (Weil am Rhein, Germany, 2019). [see images: pp. 65–9]

Wilkes, Angela, et al., *Design: The Definitive Visual History* (New York, 2015).

Woodham, Jonathan, 'Dieter Rams', *A Dictionary of Modern Design* (Oxford, 2016).

Woodhuysen, James, 'The Apostle of Cool: James Woodhuysen Profiles Dieter Rams', in *From Matt Black to Memphis and Back Again: An Anthology from Blueprint Magazine,* ed. Deyan Sudjic (London, 1989), 90–2.

LITERATURE ABOUT SPECIFIC PRODUCTS

Albus, Volker, et al., 'Braun Phonosuper SK 4: Dieter Rams und Hans Gugelot', in *Design! Das 20. Jahrhundert* (*Design! The 20th Century*) (Munich, 2000), 114–15. [see images: p. 25]

Braun AG and Jo Klatt, 'Braun Quadrophonie' ('Braun Quadrophonic Sound'), *Design+Design,* no. 23 (1992), 4–13. [see images: pp. 152, 187, 197, 213]

Butler, Nick, 'Braun Phonosuper SK Record Player: Designed by Hans Gugelot and Dieter Rams in 1956', *Design*, no. 470 (1988), 33. [see images: p. 25]

Battema, Dough, 'Gillette Company', in *The Advertising Age: Encyclopedia of Advertising,* ed. John McDonough and Karen Egolf (Chicago and London, 2002), 673–8. [see images: pp. 318–19]

Cobarg, Claus C., 'Braun Thermolüfter Linie' ('Braun Fan Heater Line'), *Design+Design,* no. 43 (1998), 8. [see images: pp. 48, 82, 123]

Cobarg, Claus C., and Dietrich Lubs, 'Wie entstand der SK 4, wer gab ihm den Namen "Schneewittchensarg"?' ('How Did the SK 4 Come About, Who Gave It the Name "Snow White's Coffin"?'), *Design+Design*, no. 87 (2009), 9–11. [see images: p. 25]

Cobarg, Claus C., Michael Unger and Peter Ziegler, 'Die Diaprojektoren von Braun' ('Braun Slide Projectors'), *Design+Design,* no. 27 (1994), 4–11.

de Lates, Thomas, 'Das Ela-Abenteuer von Braun' ('The Braun ELA Adventure'), *Design+Design*, no. 82 (2007/08), 5–11. [see images: p. 144]

'Dieter Rams was Playful with the Braun HLD 4 Hair Dryer', *European Plastics News* 41, no. 7 (2014), 31. [see images: pp. 172–3]

Fiell Charlotte and Peter, 'Dieter Rams: Model No. RZ 62', in *1000 Chairs* (Cologne, 1997), 406. [see images: p. 92]

Förderverein Schöneres Frankfurt e.V. (ed.), *Neue Standuhren im städtischen Raum* (*New Pillar Clocks for Public Spaces*) (Frankfurt am Main, 1994). [see images: p. 316]

Franksen, Inez, 'Montageprogramm 571 / 72 Vitsœ' ('Montage System 571/72 Vitsœ'), *Bauwelt,* no. 44 (1974), 1460. [see images: p. 28]

———, 'Regalsystem 606 Vitsœ Kollektion' ('Universal Shelving System 606 Vitsoe Collection'), *Bauwelt,* no. 23 (1976), 709. [see images: pp. 65–9]

Hackbarth, Andreas, 'Neu: die Arbeitstischleuchte in 3 Verstellungs-Dimensionen' ('New: The Desk Lamp in 3 Adjustment Dimensions), *Design+*

Design, no. 45 (1998), 4. [see images: pp. 328–9]

Irrek, Hans, 'Wir haben damals eine Menge über die Zusammenstellung der Dinge von ihm gelernt…' ('He Taught Us a Lot About Arranging Things…'), interview with Marlene Schnelle-Schneyder, *Design+Design*, no. 33 (1995), 24–9. [see images: p. 26]

Jatzke-Wiegand, Hartmut, 'Der Universal-empfänger T 1000 und der Universalempfänger T 1000 CD' (The T 1000 Universal Receiver and the T 1000 CD World Receiver), *Design+Design,* no. 20 (1991), 8–14. [see images: pp. 106, 137]

———, 'Konsequentes System-Design: Das Regalsystem 606 von Dieter Rams' ('Logical System Design: The Universal Shelving System 606 by Dieter Rams'), *Design+Design,* no. 60 (2002), 4–9. [see images: pp. 65–9]

Jatzke-Wiegand, Hartmut and Jo Klatt, *Design+Design* zero, 2nd edn (Hamburg, 2012).

Klatt, Jo, 'Braun HiFi – Musikanlagen Studio 46, 60, 80 und E' ('Braun HiFi – Systems Studio 46, 60, 80 and E), *Design+Design,* no. 9 (1987), 5–16. [see images: pp. 55, 75, 89, 108, 127]

———, 'Die neuen Geräte von Braun a/d/s' ('New Products from Braun a/d/s'), *Design+Design,* no. 9 (1987), 22–7. [see images: pp. 274–5]

———, 'Braun Taschenempfänger und Batterie-Plattenspieler' ('Braun Pocket Receiver and Battery-Operated Record Player'), *Design+Design,* no. 11 (1988), 4–11. [see images: pp. 42–3, 50, 51, 52, 87]

———, 'Die Radio-Phono-Kombination von Braun: SK 4 bis SK 55' ('Braun Radio-Phono Combinations: SK 4 to SK 55'), *Design+Design,* no. 15 (1989/90): 4–14. [see images: pp. 25, 38–9, 58, 109]

———, 'Das erste Braun Tonbandgerät verkörpert "ästhetisch" seine Funktion ('The First Braun Tape Recorder Stands For "Aesthetic Function")', *Design+Design,* no. 30 (1994/95), 5–21. [see images: pp. 132–3]

———, 'Das "sensible" Tonbandgerät TG 1000' ('The "Sensitive" Braun Tape Recorder TG 1000'), Design+Design, no. 37 (1996), 13–15. [see images: p. 168]

———, 'Braun Plattenspieler Teil 1: von 1955 bis 1971' ('Braun Record Players Part 1: from 1955 to 1971'), *Design+Design*, no. 38 (1996), 4–12. [see images: pp. 30, 50, 52, 76, 89, 110–11, 128, 129, 152]

———, 'Die Braun Plattenspieler Teil 2' ('Braun Record Players Part 2'), *Design+Design*, no. 39 (1997), 5–13. [see images: pp. 203, 204, 237, 239, 279]

———, 'Die Compact-Disc-Spieler zur Atelier HiFi Anlage von Braun' ('Compact Disc Players for the Atelier HiFi System by Braun'), *Design+Design,* no. 41 (1997), 5–13. [see images: p. 281]

———, 'Das "Gesicht" der Lautsprecher ('The "Faces" of Loudspeakers'), *Design+Design,* no. 42 (1997/98), 5–14. [see images: pp. 33, 37, 54, 78, 79, 98, 160, 161, 186, 229, 242, 260, 267]

———, 'Die Braun HiFi Verstärker' ('The Braun Hi-Fi Amplifiers'), *Design+Design,* no. 43 (1998): 3–7. [see images: p. 53]

———, 'Das Braun Steuergerät "regie" und seine 19 Varianten' ('The Braun "regie" Receiver and Its 19 Variants'), *Design+Design,* no. 46 (1998/99), 4–7. [see images: pp. 153, 187, 227, 250]

———, 'Neuer Stuhlentwurf von Dieter Rams'

('New Chair Design by Dieter Rams'), *Design+Design,* no. 46 (1998/99), 15. [see images: p. 331]

———, 'Die Braun Kopfhörer' ('The Braun Headphones'), *Design+Design,* no. 48 (1999), 4–6. [see images: p. 221]

———, 'Die LE 1 erlebt einen "zweiten Frühling": Der elektrostatische Lautsprecher von Braun wird in Lizenz wieder hergestellt' ('A "Second Spring" for the LE 1: Braun's Electrostatic Loudspeaker Will Be Produced Again Under Licence'), *Design+Design,* no. 50 (1999/2000), 4–7.

———, 'Dieter Rams gestaltete das offizielle Expo-Gastgeschenk' ('Dieter Rams Designed the Official Gifts for Expo Guests'), *Design+Design,* no. 52 (2000), 7. [see images: p. 330]

———, 'Die studio systeme integral: HiFi Bausteine von Braun' ('integral studio systems: The Braun Modular Hi-Fi Sound Systems'), *Design+Design,* no. 54 (2000/01), 4–8. [see images: pp. 243, 248, 249]

———, 'atelier HiFi Bausteine: Die letzten HiFi Geräte von Braun ('atelier Modular Sound Systems: The Last Braun Hi-Fi Devices'), *Design+Design,* no. 55 (2001), 4–10. [see images: pp. 274–5]

———, 'Die Braun Radios von 1955 bis 1961' ('Braun Radios from 1955 to 1961'), *Design+Design,* no. 59 (2002), 4–8. [see images: p. 73]

———, 'Braun Hi-Fi Radio-Phono-Kombinationen und die HiFi-Steuergeräte Atelier 1 bis 3' ('Braun Hi-Fi Radio-Phono combinations and the atelier 1 to 3 Hi-Fi Control Units'), *Design+Design,* no. 62 (2002/03), 4–6. [see images: pp. 32, 81]

———, 'Das besondere Einzelstück: Der Braun Kofferempfänger exporter 2 ('One of a Kind: The Braun exporter 2 Portable Radio'), *Design+Design,* no. 68 (2004), 4–6. [see images: p. 22]

———, 'Braun Studio Händler: Der "erfolgreiche" Schlussverkauf von Braun HiFi ('Braun Studio Dealers: The "Successful" Sale of Braun Hi-Fi'), *Design+Design,* no. 78 (2007), 4–7. [see images: pp. 274–5]

———, 'Braun Studioblitz-System F 1000 und F 1010' ('Braun F 1000 and F 1010 Studio Flash Systems'), *Design+Design,* no. 91 (2010), 3–5. [see images: p. 136]

Kleefisch-Joobst, Ursula (ed.), 'Dieter Rams rgs-Serie' ('Dieter Rams rgs Series'), in *Architektur zum Anfassen: FSB Greifen und Griffe* (*Approachable Architecture: FSB Grips and Handles*) (Frankfurt am Main, 2002), 124–7. [see images: pp. 312, 313, 314]

Klemp, Klaus, 'Ein Glückskind mit einigen Vätern: Die Radio-Phono-Kombination SK 4 ('A Lucky Child With Several Fathers: The SK 4 Radio-Phono Combination'), in *Hans Gugelot: Die Architektur des Design* (*Hans Gugelot: The Architecture of Design*), ed. HfG Archiv and Museum Ulm (Stuttgart, 2020), 61–79. [see images: pp. 24, 25, 38–9, 58, 109]

Leidinger, Hermann and Jo Klatt, 'Die Braun Kofferempfänger' ('The Braun Portable Radio'), *Design+Design,* no. 26 (1993), 5–15. [see images: pp. 36, 80]

Müller, Dieter, *Alles über die Nizo* (*Everything About the Nizo*), 3rd edn (Düsseldorf, 1974). [see images: p. 115]

Plewa, Jens, 'Die Vitsœ Kollektion: Möbel von

Dieter Rams, vom Montagemöbel RZ 57 zum Montagesystem 571' ('The Vitsœ Collection: Furniture by Dieter Rams, from Assembly Furniture RZ 57 to Assembly System 571'), *Design+Design*, no. 11 (1988), 12–19. [see images: p. 28]

———, '... vom Wandregal RZ 60 zum Regalsystem 606' ('... from Wall Shelf Unit RZ 60 to Shelf System 606', *Design+Design*, no. 12 (1988/89), 23–7. [see images: pp. 65–9]

———, '... Tischprogramm 57/570' ('... Table Programme 57/570'), *Design+Design*, no. 13 (1989), 32–5. [see images: p. 27]

———, '... Korpusprogramm 710' ('... Storage Programme 710', *Design+Design*, no. 14 (1989), 10–13. [see images: p. 181]

———, '... Garderobe RZ 61; Garderobenprogramm 610' ('... Wardrobe RZ 61; Wardrobe Programme 610'), *Design+Design*, no. 15 (1989/90), 26–9. [see images: pp. 70–1]

———, '... Liegenprogramm 680; Sesselprogramm 681' ('... Daybed Programme 680; Armchair Programme 681'), *Design+Design*, no. 16 (1990), 24–7. [see images: pp. 150, 151]

———, '... Schiebetürsystem 690' ('... Folding Door System 690'), *Design+Design*, no. 17 (1990), 31–33. [see images: pp. 158–9, 312, 313, 314]

———, '... Sessel RZ 60; Sesselprogramm 601 / 602; Klappstuhl RZ 62' ('... Armchair RZ 60; Armchair Programme 601/602; Folding Chair RZ 62'), *Design+Design*, no. 18 (1991), 26–31. [see images: pp. 62, 63, 64, 90–1]

———, '... Die Sesselprogramme RZ 62 bis RZ 620' ('... Chair Programme RZ 62 to RZ 620'), *Design+Design*, no. 19 (1991), 29–31. [see images: pp. 94, 95, 96, 97]

Rams, Dieter, 'Protokoll aus der Praxis: Dieter Rams zur Designentwicklung der Ton-Kamera "Nizo 2056 sound"' ('Recording from Experience: Dieter Rams on Developing the Design of the "Nizo 2056 Sound" Film Camera'), *form*, no. 73 (1976), 43. [see images: p. 236]

———, 'Konzeption einer komplexen HiFi Anlage in Pultform' ('Conception of a Complex Hi-Fi Sound System in Console Form'), *Design+Design*, no. 89 (2009), 3–7. [see images: pp. 200, 201, 202, 203, 212]

Rudolph, Klaus, 'Die Braun Armbanduhren' ('The Braun Wristwatches'), *Design+Design*, no. 5 (1986), 9–16. [see images: p. 252]

Staeffler, Günter, Braun Feuerzeuge ('Braun Lighters'), *Design+Design*, no. 8 (1987), 6–15. [see images: pp. 149, 170, 184, 185, 207, 286, 287]

———, 'Braun Taschenrechner' ('Braun Pocket Calculators'), *Design+Design*, no. 10 (1988), 24–32. [see images: pp. 241, 288, 311]

———, 'Die Braun audio Teil 1' ('Braun audio Part 1'), *Design+Design*, no. 12 (1988/89), 4–22. [see images: p. 88, 98–9, 101, 112, 121]

———, 'Formbeständig: Küchenmaschine KM 3/ KM 32' ('Constant Form: Kitchen Machine KM 3/ KM 32'), *Design+Design*, no. 13 (1989), 16. [see images: p. 35]

———, 'Braun Audio', *Design+Design*, no. 14, (1989) 14–28. [see images: pp. 169, 201, 202, 205, 238]

———, 'Braun Kaffeemaschinen' ('Braun Coffeemakers'), *Design+Design*, no. 16 (1990), 4–15. [see images: pp. 176, 191, 300]

———, 'Griffprogamm von Dieter Rams' ('Handle Programme by Dieter Rams'), *Design+Design*, no 17 (1990), 28–30.

———, 'Das Zeit-Programm von Braun: Teil 1, Tischuhren' ('The Time Programme by Braun: Part 1, Table Clocks'), *Design+Design*, no. 28 (1994), 8– 21. [see images: pp. 179, 194, 218, 219, 226, 251, 299, 327]

———, 'Braun Trockenrasierer: Die ersten 20 Jahre' ('Braun Shavers: The First 20 Years'), *Design+Design*, no. 40 (1997), 4–14. [see images: pp. 34, 44, 59, 100, 177]

———, 'Braun Elektronenblitzgeräte: Künstliches Licht formschön verpackt' ('Braun Electronic Flash Units: Beautifully Packaged Artifical Light'), *Design+Design*, no. 44 (1998), 3–9. [see images: pp. 46, 49, 61, 113, 118, 126, 134, 136, 165]

———, 'Braun Lectron: Elektronik leicht gemacht' ('Braun Lectron: Electronics Made Easy'), *Design+Design*, no. 47 (1999), 3–6. [see images: p. 147]

———, 'Braun Rasierer: von 1970 bis heute ('Braun Shavers: from 1970 to today'), *Design+Design*, no. 53 (2000), 17–30. [see images: pp. 193, 198, 199, 264, 265, 306, 315, 324]

———, 'Braun Fernsehgeräte: vom FS 1 bis zum TV 3' ('Braun Television Sets: from the FS 1 to the TV 3'), *Design+Design*, no. 56 (2001), 5–11. [see images: pp. 120, 140, 146, 285]

———, 'Bestrahlungsgerät Braun Cosmolux HUV 1' ('Braun Cosmolux HUV 1 Light Therapy Device'), *Design+Design*, no. 59 (2002), 10. [see images: p. 117]

———, 'Eine Küchenmaschine mit System: Braun Multiwerk KM 2' ('A Kitchen Machine System: Braun Multiwerk KM 2'), *Design+Design*, no. 60 (2002), 10–13. [see images: p. 124]

———, 'Braun Zitruspressen und Entsafter' ('Braun Citrus Juicers and Juice Extractors'), Design+Design, no. 62 (2002/03), 14–17. [see images: pp. 174, 189]

———, 'Die Kofferplattenspieler von Braun' ('Braun Portable Record Players'), *Design+Design*, no. 64 (2003), 4–6. [see images: pp. 31, 77]

———, 'Die Braun Tonbandgeräte TG 60 bis TG 1020' ('The Braun Tape Recorders TG 60 to TG 1020'), *Design+Design*, no. 66 (2003/04), 4–10. [see images: pp. 132–3, 168]

———, 'Interpretation langlebigen Designs: Braun Kaffeemühlen' ('Interpretation of Durable Designs: Braun Coffee Grinders'), *Design+Design*, no. 67 (2004), 3–7. [see images: p. 157, 175]

———, 'Die Uhrenradios von Braun' ('The Braun Clock Radios'), *Design+Design*, no. 71 (2005), 11–15. (see images: pp. 254–5, 289)

———, 'Das Gesamtprogramm der Braun Nizo Filmprojektoren' ('The Complete Braun Nizo Film Projector Series'), *Design+Design*, no.73 (2005), 4–10. [see images: p. 119]

———, 'Braun energetic: Das Tischfeuerzeug mit Solarzellen' ('Braun energetic: Table Lighters with Solar Cells'), *Design+Design*, no. 76, (2006), 10. [see images: pp. 208–9]

———, 'Braun Handrührer' ('Braun Hand Mixers'), *Design+Design*, no. 80 (2007), 14–17. [see images: pp. 60, 124, 156]

———, 'Die Tonarmwaage' ('The Track Force Gauge'), *Design+Design*, no 80 (2007), 18. [see images: p. 86]

———, 'Braun Design für Schreibgeräte von Paper Mate' ('Braun Design for Paper Mate Writing Instruments'), *Design+Design*, no. 81 (2007), 8. [see images: pp. 214, 215]

———, 'Braun Design-Studien' ('Braun Design Studies'), *Design+Design*, no. 79 (2007), 3–12. [see images: pp. 103, 164, 166, 167, 230, 231, 272, 290, 302]

———, 'Gillette octagon', *Design+Design*, no. 81 (2007), 10. [see images: pp. 296, 297]

———, 'Personenwaage und Messlatte von Braun' ('Braun Bathroom Scales and Measuring Rod'), *Design+Design*, no. 85 (2008), 13. [see images: p. 155]

———, 'Die Cassettenrecorder von Braun' ('Braun Cassette Recorders'), *Design+Design*, no. 87, (2009), 3–5. [see images: pp. 220, 257, 278]

———, 'Das Tischfeuerzeug Braun cylindric: Original und Neuproduktionen' ('The Braun Cylindric Table Lighter: Original and New Productions'), *Design+Design*, no. 87 (2009), 12. [see images: p. 149]

———, 'Die Taschenrechner von Braun: Das gesamte Programm von 1975 bis 2004 ('The Braun Pocket Calculators: The Complete Series from 1975 to 2004'), *Design+Design*, no. 90 (2009/10), 3–10. [see images: pp. 222, 228, 241, 261, 288, 310, 311, 326]

———, 'Die Braun Armbanduhren: Übersicht, von der DW 20 bis zur AW 200' ('The Braun Wristwatches: Overview, from the DW 20 to the AW 200'), *Design+Design*, no. 91 (2010), 7–11. [see images: pp. 317, 325]

Staeffler, Günter and Jo Klatt, 'Zeitzeichen: Innovatives Uhren-Design von Braun' ('Sign of the Times: Innovative Clock and Watch Design by Braun'), *Design+Design*, no. 77 (2006), 11. [see images: pp. 240, 251, 252, 309, 317, 322–3, 327]

Unger, Michael and Peter Ziegler, 'Die Diaprojektoren von Braun' ('The Braun Slide Projectors'), *Design+Design*, no. 27 (1993/94), 4–11. [see images: pp. 23, 47, 72, 83, 84, 85, 171]

Witke, Boris, 'Braun SK 4: Die erste Kompaktanlage, Funkgeschichte' ('Braun SK 4: The First Compact Systems, Radio History'), *Design+Design*, no. 241 (2018), 228–39. [see images: pp. 25, 38–9, 58, 109]

Wittorf, Susanne, 'Zeitloser Entwurf: Lamp by Dieter Rams, RHa 1/2' ('Timeless Design: Lamp by Dieter Rams RHa 1/2'), *design report*, no. 7 (1998), 14 and 92. [see images: pp. 328–9]

Yadin, Daniel L., *Creative Marketing Communications: A Practical Guide to Planning, Skills and Techniques*, 3rd edn (London, 2001) [see images: pp. 318–19]

Ziegler, Peter, 'Nizo: Die Kameramarke von Braun' ('Nizo: The Braun Camera Brand'), *Design+Design*, no. 10 (1988), 4–18. [see images: 114, 115, 135]

Ziegler, Peter, 'Nizo: Die Kameramarke von Braun, Superachtfilmkameras der kleinen Baureihe ('Nizo: The Braun Camera Brand, Super-8 movie camera without sound recording of the small series'), *Design+Design*, no. 11 (1988), 22–8. [see images: pp. 206, 236]

———, 'Nizo: Die Kameramarke von Braun, Tonfilmkameras' ('Nizo: The Braun Camera Brand, sound film cameras'), *Design+Design*, no. 13 (1989), 22–31. [see images: p. 266]

DIETER RAMS BIOGRAPHY

20 May 1932
Born in Wiesbaden. Early experience with cabinetmaking, influenced by his grandfather who was a master cabinetmaker

9 April–30 September 1947
Begins studies in architecture and interior design at the Kunstgewerbeschule (School of Arts) Wiesbaden

September 1947
Studies interrupted to begin apprenticeship in cabinetmaking; obtains a journeyman's licence; meets Gerd A Müller while at vocational college. Wins the district craft competition in November 1951 with a sideboard for a dining room

October 1951
Resumes studies at the Kunstgewerbeschule Wiesbaden, which had been reformed by Dr Hans Soeder to become the Werkkunstschule (School of Applied Arts)

July 1953
Graduates with honours for the design of a banking hall

October 1953–July 1955
Works at the Otto Apel architectural firm in Frankfurt; collaborates with the US architecture firm Skidmore, Owings & Merrill on the construction of the US consulate buildings in Frankfurt and Bremen

15 July 1955
Employed at Max Braun oHG, Frankfurt, as an interior designer

Early 1956
Creates first works as a product designer (PA 1 and, together with Hans Gugelot, SK 4)

1956
First furniture designs; meets Otto Zapf

July–September 1957
Exhibition of numerous new Braun devices (above all, the SK 4) presented in show apartments at the Internationale Bauausstellung (International Building Exhibition, or Interbau) 1957 in Berlin

July–November 1957
Wins the Grand Prix award at the eleventh Milan Triennale for the overall Braun range (including SK 1/2, exporter 2, PA 1, SK 4 and transistor 1)

April–October 1958
Presentation of sixteen new Braun devices at Expo 58 (World's Fair) in Brussels

December 1958–February 1959
Five Braun appliances, designed by Dieter Rams, in collaboration with Hans Gugelot and Gerd A Müller, are added to the permanent collection of the Museum of Modern Art (MoMA) in New York and shown in the *20th Century Design from the Museum Collection* exhibition (SK 5, transistor 2, PA 2, KM 3 and T 3)

1960
Awarded the Stipendium des Kulturkreises bursary by the Bundesverband der Deutschen Industrie (National Association of German Industry)

May 1961
After its establishment in 1959, Vitsoe+Zapf is legally registered as a company for the production and distribution of furniture designs by Dieter Rams

1961
Appointed head of the Braun AG product design department

1961 and 1963
Presented with the Supreme Award of the *Interplas* exhibition in London for the products TP 1 (awarded 1961) and F 21 (awarded 1963)

1965
Receives the Junge Generation Berlin Art Award for Industrial Design, together with Reinhold Weiss, Richard Fischer and Robert Oberheim

1968
Appointed Director of Product Design at Braun AG

June 1968
Awarded the title of Honorary Royal Designer for Industry (Hon. RDI) by the Royal Society of Arts, London, for his outstanding design in the field of furniture and technical products

April 1971
Made a Fellow of the Royal Society of Arts, London

October 1973
Presentation of the Braun design philosophy at the International Council of Societies of Industrial Design (ICSID) congress in Kyoto, together with Fritz Eichler and Wolfgang Schmittel

September 1977
Appointment to the executive committee of the Rat für Formgebung (German Design Council)

January 1978
Awarded the SIAD Medal by the Society of Industrial Artists and Designers, London

28 November 1980
Opening of the *Dieter Rams &* exhibition at the International Design Centre (IDZ) in Berlin, which travels to: Biennale of Industrial Design, Ljubljana, 1981; Amos Andersen Art Museum, Helsinki, 1981; Padiglione d'Arte Contemporanea, Milan, 1981; Victoria and Albert Museum, London, 1982; Stedelijk Museum, Amsterdam, 1982; Museum of Decorative Arts, Cologne, 1983

7 November 1981
Appointed Professor of Industrial Design at the Hochschule für bildende Künste (University of Fine Arts), Hamburg

October 1983–January 1984
Takes part in the *Design since 1945* exhibition at the Philadelphia Museum of Art

1984
Aluminium version of the Universal Shelving System 606 produced by De Padova, Milan

1985
Made Académico de Honor Extranjero (Honorary Foreign Academician) by the Academia Mexicana de Diseño, Mexico City

1986
Appointed honorary member of the International Faculty, Ontario College of Art, Toronto

November 1987
Honorary member of Verband Deutscher Industrie Designer (Association of German Industrial Designers)

1987–1998
President of the German Design Council, honorary member since 2002

1988
Appointed Executive Director of Braun AG

1989
Braun design department named Design Team of the Year by Haus Industrieform, Essen

April–June 1989
Good Offices: The Seventh Arango International Design Exhibition, juror Dieter Rams, together with the *Dieter Rams* retrospective exhibition, Museum of Art, Fort Lauderdale, Florida, which travels to: ArtCenter College of Design, Pasadena, California, 1990; Musée des Arts Décoratifs, Montreal, 1990

August 1990
Becomes the first recipient of the Industrie Forum (iF) Design Award for his special services to design

5 July 1991
Awarded an honorary doctorate (Doctor Honoris Causa) by the Royal College of Art, London

1992
Receives the IKEA Prize; uses the prize money to establish the Dieter and Ingeborg Rams Foundation to promote design

1993–1995
Member of the ICSID executive board

1995
Title changed from Director of Product Design to Executive Director of Corporate Identity Affairs at Braun AG

1996
Awarded the World Design Medal by the Industrial Designers Society of America

June 1997
Awarded the Hessian Order of Merit

1997
Retired from Braun AG

1997
Emeritus professor of the Hochschule für bildende Künste (University of Fine Arts), Hamburg

May 1999
Appointed a member of the Akademie der Künste (Academy of Arts), Berlin

May–August 2001
Tingens Stilla Ordning exhibition opens at the Skissernas Museum, Lund, Sweden

September–November 2001
Dieter Rams House exhibition opens at the Centro de Exposicoés Centro Cultural de Belém, Lisbon, Portugal

October–November 2002
Dieter Rams Design: The Fascination of the Simple exhibition opens at the Institut für Neue Technische Form, Darmstadt, which travels to: Wilhelm Wagenfeld House, Bremen

October 2002
Awarded the Grand Cross of the Order of Merit of the Federal Republic of Germany

October 2002–January 2003
Dieter Rams – Less But Better exhibition opens at the Museum Angewandte Kunst (Museum of Applied Art), Frankfurt am Main

June 2004
Awarded the ONDI Design Prize for outstanding contributions to industrial design and world culture, Havana

September–October 2005
Dieter Rams – Less But Better exhibition opens at the Kenninji (Zen) Temple, Kyoto

October 2005
Receives the Diploma de Reconocimiento (award acknowledging his significant contribution to the development of design in Latin America) from the Asociación Latinoamericana de Diseño (ALADI), Buenos Aires. Receives the Busse Longlife Design Award for the MPZ 22 citromatic deluxe citrus juicer, together with Jürgen Greubel

February 2007
Receives the Design Award of the Federal Republic of Germany for his life's work

May–July 2007
Design: Dieter Rams exhibition opens at the State Museum of Ceramics, Kuskovo Estate, Moscow

November 2007
Receives the Raymond Loewy Foundation's Lucky Strike Designer Award

November 2008–January 2009
Less and More. The Design Ethos of Dieter Rams travelling exhibition opens at the Suntory Museum, Osaka, which travels to: Fuchu Art Museum, Tokyo, 2009; the Design Museum, London, 2009–10; Museum Angewandte Kunst, Frankfurt am Main, 2010; Daelim Museum, Seoul, 2010–11; San Francisco Museum of Modern Art (SFMoMA), 2011–12

May 2010
Receives the Kölner Klopfer Award, KISD, Cologne International School of Design

November 2011
Receives the Hessian Cultural Award, together with Prof. FC Gundlach and Prof. Gunter Rambow

July 2012
Named Distinguished Affiliated Professor at the Technische Universität München (Technical University of Munich)

November 2012
Receives the Moholy-Nagy award, Moholy-Nagy University for Art and Design (MOME), Budapest

April 2013
Awarded an Honorary Doctorate of Arts, ArtCenter College of Design, Pasadena, California

September 2013
Receives the London Design Medal Lifetime Achievement Award

May 2014
Receives the Premio Compasso d'Oro ADI alla Carriera Internazionale (Award for Lifetime Achievement) from the ADI Milan

November 2016–March 2017
Dieter Rams: Modular World exhibition opens at the Vitra Design Museum, Weil am Rhein

September 2018
Premiere of the documentary film *Rams* (74 minutes), at the SVA Theatre in New York; produced and directed by Gary Hustwit, original music by Brian Eno

November 2018–April 2019
Dieter Rams: Principled Design exhibition opens at the Philadelphia Museum of Art

EDITORIAL SOURCE NOTES

The author has compiled all technical and formal information on the objects to the best of his knowledge and belief, although no legal guarantee can be given.

The explanations reflect the author's view, but are based on numerous archival sources and interviews, and they have been discussed with Dieter Rams.

The information and chronological classifications of the Braun devices are based on the many years of work carried out by the collectors' magazine *Design+Design* and the publication *Braun+Design* Collection, edited by Jo Klatt and Günter Staeffler (Hamburg, 2nd edition, 1995). New findings were supplemented or corrected accordingly.

The majority of product dimensions have been remeasured. Where this was not possible, the measurements are based on the book *Less and More: The Design Ethos of Dieter Rams* (Berlin, 2009), company catalogues and other sources.

The Braun employee magazine *Betriebsspiegel* from 1962 to 1995 was also used as a reference for measurements and prices.

The objects for the photographs made by Andreas Kugel were kindly provided by the Museum Angewandte Kunst (Museum of Applied Arts), Frankfurt am Main; the Braun Collection, Kronberg im Taunus; Dieter Rams; and private collectors. Further photographic sources are listed in the picture credits.

For the Braun and Vitsœ products, original sales prices in German deutschmarks (DM) were taken from the companies' respective sales catalogues at the time and also from the *Braun+Design Tax List* (Hamburg, 9th ed, 2017), as well as from the website of the Schweizer Radiomuseum (radiomuseum.org). Where later prices are given, this is indicated. The original retail prices could not be determined for all objects. At the time of writing, DM 1 is equal to: EUR€0.51; GBP£0.46; and USD$0.57

The author has made every effort to locate all other owners of reproduction rights. Persons and institutions who may not have been reached and who claim rights to any utilized images are requested to contact the publisher.

Phaidon Press Limited
2 Cooperage Yard
London E15 2QR

Phaidon Press Inc.
111 Broadway
New York, NY 10006

phaidon.com

First published 2020
Reprinted 2021 (twice), 2022, 2024
© 2020 Phaidon Press Limited

ISBN 978 1 83866 153 3

A CIP catalogue record for this
book is available from the British
Library and the Library of Congress.

Commissioning Editor: Emilia Terragni
Project Editor: Robyn Taylor
Production Controllers:
Abigail Draycott, Elaine Ward
Design: Order

Printed in China

PICTURE CREDITS
Unless otherwise stated, all photography is
courtesy Andreas Kugel

Appel Design Gallery, Studio Christoph Sagel:
92–3; Florian Böhm: 182; Ingeborg Kracht-Rams:
27–9, 62–3, 90–1, 150–1, 158–9, 180–1, 183, 195;
Marlene Schnelle-Schneyder: 26

COPYRIGHT CREDITS
Unless otherwise stated, all images are courtesy
and © copyright Dieter Rams Archive.

BRAUN P&G, Braun Archive Kronberg: 22,
24–5, 36, 40, 42–3, 48–50, 52–3, 55, 58, 60,
72–3, 80, 85, 89, 103–5, 108, 110–11, 124, 132–3,
138, 141–2, 144, 170, 172–3, 177–8, 191, 218–19,
225, 228, 235, 263, 265, 274–5, 303, 317, 324,
326; Fotoarchiv Jo Klatt D+D Verlag, Hamburg:
47, 76–7, 107, 134, 158–9, 213, 231, 260, 298;
Günter Staeffler, Kirchbrak: 122; Vitsœ Ltd.:
65–9, 92–3, 210–11, 304

COLLECTIONS
Unless otherwise stated, all works are part of
the Braun collection on permanent loan from
BRAUN P&G to the Museum Angewandte Kunst
(Museum of Applied Arts), Frankfurt am Main

Braun Sammlung, Kronberg / Ts.: 24, 59, 64, 79,
82–4, 89, 108, 112, 116, 119, 120, 127, 128–31, 137,
139, 140, 142, 144, 152–3, 155, 161, 188, 197–9,
203, 207, 221, 229, 237–9, 241–3, 250, 262, 264,
267, 277, 280–1, 287–9, 291–2, 299, 301, 303,
308, 324, 326; Museum Angewandte Kunst,
Frankfurt am Main, gift of Dieter Rams: 94–5, 148,
192, 208–9, 307, 312–14, 316, 333–5; Museum
Angewandte Kunst, Frankfurt am Main, gift of
Marlene Schnelle-Schneyder: 26

PUBLISHER'S ACKNOWLEDGEMENTS

The publisher would like to thank Klaus Klemp,
Dieter Rams and Britte Siepenkothen for their
generosity and patience during the making
of this book, and Juan Aranda, Robert Davies,
João Mota, Anthony Naughton, Jesse Reed,
Ariane Sagiadinos and Jonathan Whale for
their valuable contributions.